DATE DUE

"Wh   eople
with   with
chilc   o get
invo   who
have   suggest   o get
thei   ets in
thei

                                                       1ator,
                                                        and
                                                       nent,

"Thi   d the
asse

                                                       Ways

"*What Young Children Need to Succeed* is an invaluable tool for all members in our community—parents, caregivers, employers, community leaders, librarians, educators, medical providers—to help children bloom into healthy, caring adults. The 40 key factors identified, with more than 1,000 creative ideas for working with infants, toddlers, preschoolers, and elementary-age children, reinforce and promote each other—just as we need to work together. I wholeheartedly recommend this book!"

—*Hilary Pert Stecklein, M.D., FAAP, Pediatrician and Founder of Reading RX*

"This book elicits actions! And one caring adult *can* make a difference in the lives of children."

—*Marilyn Peplau, Guidance Counselor, School District of New Richmond, New Richmond, Wisconsin*

What Young Children Need to Succeed

Working Together to Build Assets from Birth to Age 11

Jolene L. Roehlkepartain
and Nancy Leffert, Ph.D.

free spirit
PUBLiSHiNG®

Works
for kids™

Library of Congress Cataloging-in-Publication Data
Roehlkepartain, Jolene L., 1962–
     What young children need to succeed : working together to build assets from birth to age 11 / by Jolene L. Roehlkepartain and Nancy Leffert.
       p.   cm.
     Includes bibliographical references and index.
     ISBN 1-57542-070-8 (pbk.)
     1. Child rearing. 2. Moral education. 3. Altruism in children.
  I. Leffert, Nancy, 1949– . II. Title.
  HQ769.R617 2000
  649'.1—dc21   99-37224
                                                           CIP

Cover design by Percolator
Illustrations by Marieka Heinlen
Book design and layout by Jessica Thoreson
Index prepared by Kay Schlembach

What Young Children Need to Succeed is based on *Starting Out Right: Developmental Assets for Children* by Nancy Leffert, Ph.D., Peter L. Benson, Ph.D., and Jolene L. Roehlkepartain, published in 1997 by Search Institute as part of Search Institute's national Healthy Communities • Healthy Youth Initiative, with support provided by Lutheran Brotherhood.

Note: This book contains many recommendations for Web sites. Because Web sites change often and without notice, we can't promise every address listed will still be accurate when you read it. When in doubt, use a search engine.

10 9 8 7 6 5 4 3 2 1
Printed in the United States of America

Free Spirit Publishing Inc.
400 First Avenue North, Suite 616
Minneapolis, MN 55401-1724
(612) 338-2068
help4kids@freespirit.com
www.freespirit.com

DEDICATION

To our families—
Gene, Micah, and Linnea Roehlkepartain
Mark, Jonathan, and Jeremy Leffert
and to all the children who have touched our lives.

ACKNOWLEDGMENTS

We thank Rebecca Grothe; Brenda Holben; Kay Hong; Irv Katz; Kathleen Kimball-Baker; Mary Nelson; Amy O'Leary; Gayle Olson; Barbara Pearce; Marilyn Peplau; Hilary Pert Stecklein, M.D.; Lesia Pikaart; Eugene Roehlkepartain; Amy Susman-Stillman, Ph.D.; Sandra Swanson; Terri Swanson; Nancy Tellett-Royce; Elanah Toporoff; and Cindy Wilcox for their careful review of earlier drafts of this book. We thank Amanda Seigel and Renee Vraa for their assistance in the preparation of this book. In addition, we are grateful to Amy Susman-Stillman, Ph.D., who helped to broaden and deepen how we have defined the developmental assets for children. Finally, we appreciate the thoughtful editorial work of Kathleen Kimball-Baker at Search Institute and the editorial team at Free Spirit Publishing: Judy Galbraith, Pamela Espeland, Marjorie Lisovskis, Jessica Thoreson, and Darsi Dreyer.

Major support for Search Institute's work on developmental assets is provided by Lutheran Brotherhood, a not-for-profit organization providing financial services and community service opportunities for Lutherans worldwide. Additional support is provided by the Colorado Trust, Dewitt-Wallace Reader's Digest Fund, W.K. Kellogg Foundation, and others.

CONTENTS

INTRODUCTION

We've all heard about children who visit elderly cancer patients in hospitals. Children who give their favorite stuffed animals to young people who lost everything in a natural disaster. Children who have positive values and a sense of purpose, who get along with each other and the adults in their lives, who have the strength to resist negative pressures and influences. We admire these children, and we'd like our children to be like them. But how?

Search Institute has been exploring this question for some time. Since 1989, its researchers have surveyed young people in communities across the country to learn what helps children grow up healthy, caring, and productive. Almost 100,000 young people in grades 6 through 12 have shared information about themselves and their lives since the surveys began.*

After studying the results, researchers identified 40 key factors that make a powerful difference in young people's lives. These factors are called **developmental assets.** They include things like family support, a caring neighborhood, self-esteem, and resistance skills. The *more* assets young people have, the *more* likely they are to become caring, competent, contributing adults, and the *less* likely they are to lose their way and get into trouble.

It's reasonable to expect that if assets are good for young people ages 12 and up, they're also good for younger children. Most child development experts agree that children need to start out right from day one. Given a healthy beginning and a firm foundation, children can develop their full potential and make the assets a part of their lives. Those who have many assets when they're young are more likely to hang on to them as they grow. Caring adults can build assets in even the youngest child.

ABOUT THIS BOOK

What Young Children Need to Succeed gives you more than 1,000 practical, creative ideas for building all 40 assets in children from

---

* This book is based in part on information from Search Institute's surveys of 99,462 young people in grades 6–12 during the 1996–97 school year, the most current information available at the time of publication.

birth to age 11. These are things that anyone can do—parents, educators, community leaders. You don't need special training or expertise, and you can start right away—today, if you want.

The assets are grouped into eight categories:

1. Support
2. Empowerment
3. Boundaries and Expectations
4. Constructive Use of Time
5. Commitment to Learning
6. Positive Values
7. Social Competencies
8. Positive Identity

Each group begins with a definition of the category, a list of the assets the category includes, and information about how many of the 6th graders Search Institute surveyed reported having each asset in their lives.

Why include information about 6th graders here, since this book is about younger children?* Because it tells you what young people that age have learned—and *not* learned. And it gives you insight into areas of greatest need. For example, only 20 percent of 6th graders perceive that adults in their community value young people. This tells us all that we need to work especially hard on building Asset 7: Community Values Children.

Each asset has its own chapter. Each chapter begins with a general definition of the asset, followed by specific definitions for four age groups: **infants** (birth to 12 months), **toddlers** (13 to 35 months), **preschoolers** (ages 3 to 5), and **elementary-age children** (ages 6 to 11).** Sometimes the definitions are the same for all four groups; sometimes they're different. Immediately after the definitions, you'll find ideas for building assets for all children, then ideas for helping children in each of the four age groups.

---

* For more on this topic, see "The Power of Developmental Assets" (pages 8–12).

** For at-a-glance lists of all the definitions, see "The Assets Defined" (pages 13–23).

You'll also read about ways specific groups can build assets in children. We've included suggestions for **parents, childcare providers, educators, health-care professionals, congregational leaders, employers, librarians,** and **community leaders.** Some of these people (parents, childcare providers, educators) have special relationships with children; the tips can help you make the most of the time you spend together. Others (health-care professionals, congregational leaders, employers, librarians, community leaders) have a powerful impact on children's lives; the tips can guide you to think more purposefully about children as you set policies and make decisions. We've also included tips for children themselves, written in simple language. We invite you to copy these tips and give them to a child you know.

Throughout the book, "Did You Know?" sections feature interesting facts about building assets and related topics. "Assets in Action" profile people who are building assets at home and in their communities, on their own and in groups. "Resource" notes direct you to books, magazines, organizations, and Web sites we recommend.

The "Resources" list on pages 296–304 points you toward more information about understanding children at different ages. We've also included books and other materials that give further details about assets and asset building. This information is helpful for anyone who works with children.

ABOUT THE LANGUAGE USED IN THIS BOOK

We use the words *parent* and *parents* to refer to children's primary caregivers. Of course, not all children live with two biological parents, or even with one. But rather than list all the possibilities (guardians, stepparents, foster parents, grandparents, etc.), we use *parent/parents* to keep things simple. If you're an adult who's caring for a child, *parent* means *you.*

We use *congregation* to describe a place where people gather for religious services, whether it's a church, temple, synagogue, mosque, or meeting house. Asset building is important in all faith communities, and we mean *congregation* to include everyone.

The asset definitions are given in very precise language. Some may seem formal or academic. This is because they're based on research, and the language of research is specific. In fact, the assets are really quite simple to understand, and the more experience you have with them, the clearer they become. If you get stuck on a definition, look at the tips.

You'll notice that the language of the asset definitions takes into account how children grow and change. For example, infants observe their world; toddlers tackle it. Infants stay in relatively close quarters; toddlers take off. Infants interact with their caregivers; toddlers get into everything. Young infants take in their world through observation; older infants and toddlers still do a lot of watching, but they also begin to connect more with others and actively explore what's around them. The ability to move on their own opens up new experiences for them.

Preschoolers are starting to take a more active role in the world. Children between ages 3 and 5 are learning that their actions affect other people. They begin to make simple choices and enjoy doing things that challenge their thinking and physical coordination. Their rapidly growing language skills help them develop in new ways.

Elementary-age children spend less time at home, and people outside the family have a greater influence on them. Their verbal skills and reasoning ability expand. They begin to make many of the assets a part of themselves and develop them on their own— provided they have asset-building adults in their lives.

If you're familiar with the asset framework for older children and teenagers,* you'll notice that *What Young Children Need to Succeed* defines some of the assets in slightly different ways.** The assets for adolescents include 20 *external* assets (things adults provide for them) and 20 *internal* assets (things that come from the inside). Because young children aren't yet able to internalize assets, all 40 assets are presented here as *external*. For example, Asset 26: Caring (for adolescents) becomes Asset 26: Family Values Caring (for young children). Adolescents can learn and

---

* This framework is described in *What Kids Need to Succeed* and *What Teens Need to Succeed* by Peter L. Benson, Judy Galbraith, and Pamela Espeland (for more information about these books and for additional resources on the asset framework, see "Resources," pages 296–304).

** The authors, along with Search Institute President Peter L. Benson, Ph.D., wrote the report *Starting Out Right: Developmental Assets for Children,* which introduced the concept of children's assets and outlined research studies that have been conducted in areas that represent each of the 40 developmental assets.

practice caring on their own. Younger children develop a sense of caring when they are cared for and taught by others how to care.

Except for some language changes, the 40 assets in this book are very similar to (and, in many cases, identical to) the assets for adolescents. If you know that framework, you already know a lot about this one.

How to Use This Book

The tips and ideas in *What Young Children Need to Succeed* will work for anyone who's involved with children in any way. The scope is broad because all children need *everyone* to be an asset builder.

Individual children develop at different rates, so use the age ranges (infant, toddler, preschooler, elementary-age) as guidelines, not hard-and-fast rules.

Some parts of this book are aimed at specific audiences. For example, Asset 1: Family Support and Asset 2: Positive Family Communication focus mainly on what parents and family members can do. This doesn't mean you can't build that asset if you're not a parent. You can help by supporting other parents and creating an environment where it's easy for parents to build assets.

Many asset definitions for very young children (infants, toddlers, and preschoolers) focus on what parents or other primary caregivers can do. Again, any caring adult can and should build these assets. (Look at the suggestions under "All Children" to learn basic ways.) Especially when a family has more than one child, it's important to have other adults around to offer support, guidance, and time off when the parents need it.

As you read this book, use the ideas that appeal to you the most—the ones that best fit your style and situation. If you don't have much time or experience with children, try some of the simpler tips first. What's important is to *start somewhere*. Say hello to a neighborhood child you know. Send a birthday card to a child of a friend or relative. Any act of asset building, however small it may seem, can make a difference. To make an even bigger difference, join with people around you and build assets together.

You'll discover that the assets are connected. As you start building one, you'll build others at the same time. For example, when you care for an infant, you're building Asset 1: Family Support and Asset 7: Community Values Children. Coaching a 4th-grade basketball team builds Asset 3: Other Adult Relationships, Asset 18: Out-of-Home Activities, Asset 21: Achievement Expectation and Motivation, and more. You'll notice other connections, too.

As you work to build assets, keep these ideas in mind:

1. Asset building is for all children, and all children need assets. While it's especially important to build assets in children who are in crisis or who have special needs, all children can use more assets. This means children with learning differences, "average" children, and gifted children. Children who like sports or books or music. Children who have many friends or no friends. Children from all socioeconomic groups. Every child needs your support and care.

2. Relationships are essential. You don't have to lead a scout troop to build assets (although you can certainly build assets there, too). What's most important is forming a relationship with a child. You can do this informally (for example, by getting to know your niece) or formally (by becoming an assistant soccer coach or reading to children at story hour at the library). What if you don't have many children in your life? You can reach out to the children of adults you know. Make a point of connecting and building relationships with them.

3. Everyone can build assets. This includes you! It includes all of us, even those who don't know much about children or haven't spent much time with children before. Again, you don't need much (or any) experience with children. Start small or work behind the scenes. Donate books to a childcare center. Make props and costumes for an elementary school play. Do whatever you can to help children feel like an important part of your community.

4. Building assets is an ongoing process. Even before a child joins the family, parents can learn the basics of asset building to make their home a welcoming place. Child development experts agree that it's important for a child to have a strong foundation for the first three years. That foundation needs to be reinforced, shaped, and expanded as the child grows—through childhood, adolescence, and into adulthood.

5. Asset building requires consistent messages. Families, schools, and communities need to work together to build assets in children. Everyone can let children know that they're important and special. When children have support from people throughout the community, positive messages come through with greater strength. For example, parents and teachers can work together to let children know that they're worthwhile people.

6. Duplication and repetition are important. In a society that emphasizes efficiency, this isn't always easy to do. Children need asset-building experiences every day and in every setting. It's impossible to give children too many assets or provide too many asset-building opportunities. When children hear something over and over, they'll start to believe it and make it a part of themselves as they grow.

TELL US YOUR IDEAS

We welcome your suggestions and ideas for building assets in children. And we'd love to hear your success stories. You can write to us at this address:

> **What Young Children Need to Succeed**
> c/o Free Spirit Publishing Inc.
> 400 First Avenue North, Suite 616
> Minneapolis, MN 55401-1724
> Email: help4kids@freespirit.com

It's our hope that building assets will become a national effort—that every person in every community will work to create a better world and a positive future for all children.

JOLENE L. ROEHLKEPARTAIN
NANCY LEFFERT, PH.D.

THE POWER OF DEVELOPMENTAL ASSETS

Every child is unique. You'll notice this right away when you step into a toddler room at a childcare center or watch a neighborhood basketball game. Some children pay attention; others are in their own world. Some hug their friends; others may slug them. And although all children can have good days and bad days, some children stand out. These aren't always the brightest or the happiest (or the crankiest), but the ones who act in positive ways.

We believe that these children have things other children don't. They have support from their parents, other adults, and their peers. They have boundaries that guide them, and appropriate expectations that encourage them to develop new skills. They're comfortable being themselves. They have meaningful ways to spend their time, and many opportunities to explore and learn. These children also have positive values, social skills, and a positive identity.

In other words, these children have *developmental assets* and people in their lives who are helping them build and strengthen the assets.

The assets are amazingly powerful. By surveying nearly 100,000 6th to 12th graders in communities across the country, Search Institute has learned just how powerful they are.

For example, the *more* assets a young person has, the *less* likely he or she is to use alcohol. Among 6th to 12th graders with 10 or fewer assets, 65 percent report using alcohol—compared to 7 percent of young people with 31 to 40 assets. The findings for smoking are similar. Young people with more assets are less likely to smoke.

In fact, Search Institute researchers have found positive connections between the assets and 24 risky behaviors. (See Table 1, page 9.)

It's also true that the more assets young people have, the more likely they are to grow up doing positive things that society values. For example, only 6 percent of 6th to 12th graders with 10 or fewer assets are likely to avoid doing risky things—compared to 43 percent of young people with 31 to 40 assets. The findings are similar

THE MORE ASSETS YOUNG PEOPLE HAVE, THE LESS LIKELY THEY ARE TO:

1. use alcohol
2. binge drink
3. smoke
4. use smokeless tobacco
5. use inhalants
6. use marijuana
7. use other illicit drugs
8. become depressed
9. attempt suicide
10. shoplift
11. vandalize
12. gamble
13. hit someone
14. hurt someone
15. use a weapon
16. participate in group fighting
17. have sexual intercourse
18. carry a weapon for protection
19. threaten to physically harm someone
20. skip school
21. get into trouble with the police
22. develop an eating disorder
23. ride with a driver who is intoxicated
24. drink and drive while under the influence

Table 1

for eight positive, thriving behaviors Search Institute examined. (See Table 2, page 10.)

The youngest children in Search Institute's surveys are in 6th grade. Obviously, we've made some leaps to translate that knowledge into ideas for building assets in younger children. To make sure our ideas are accurate and reasonable, we've consulted experts in child development and studied scientific research.*

---

* In 1997, Search Institute published a summary of what we learned in *Starting Out Right: Developmental Assets for Children* by Nancy Leffert, Ph.D., Peter L. Benson, Ph.D., and Jolene Roehlkepartain. For more information, see "Resources" (pages 296–304).

THE MORE ASSETS YOUNG PEOPLE HAVE, THE MORE LIKELY THEY ARE TO:

1. succeed in school by getting mostly A's
2. help friends or neighbors for at least one hour per week
3. value getting to know people of many racial/ethnic groups
4. pay attention to healthy nutrition and exercise
5. avoid doing dangerous things
6. be a leader of a group in the past year
7. save money instead of spending it right away
8. refuse to give up when things get difficult

Table 2

Here are some other important things Search Institute learned from the surveys:

Younger adolescents tend to have more assets than older teenagers. Sixth graders report a higher average number of assets than 11th graders. This suggests that children have fewer assets as they grow older—and underscores the importance of giving young children a strong foundation of assets as early as we can.

Some assets may weaken over the years. For example, while 71 percent of 6th graders report having Asset 31: Restraint, only 21 percent of 12th graders report this asset—a difference of 50 percent. Asset 12: School Boundaries has a similar pattern; while 70 percent of 6th graders report having this asset, only 34 percent of 12th graders do.* If we concentrate on building assets in young children, they might begin adolescence better prepared for the challenges of the teenage years.

---

* In *What Young Children Need to Succeed,* Asset 31 is Family Values Healthy Lifestyle, and Asset 12 is Out-of-Home Boundaries. "About the Language Used in This Book" (pages 3–5) explains why some assets have different definitions.

Children may not have enough assets. The average 6th grader surveyed had 21.5 of the 40 developmental assets. Only 15 percent of 6th graders report 31 to 40 assets. We can't expect all children to have all of the assets all of the time, but 31 out of 40 might be a reasonable goal.

We need to take young children's risky behaviors seriously. It's tempting to dismiss some inappropriate childhood behaviors because they don't seem frightening or dangerous. But some behaviors may be warning signs of problems that need to be addressed. (Table 3, below, shows the top five risky behaviors reported by 6th graders in Search Institute's surveys.)

There can be a fine line between normal childhood "problems" and behaviors that require serious parental concern or even professional intervention. All children, at some time or another, will hit someone else. It's not unusual to hear an angry young child shout, "I hate you!" or "I wish you were dead!" Although putting such feelings into words is better than hitting, physical and verbal attacks may signal that children haven't yet learned how to express their emotions appropriately or how to cope in positive ways with difficult situations. When we observe a young

THE TOP FIVE RISKY BEHAVIORS REPORTED BY 6TH GRADERS ARE:

1. hitting someone (44 percent of 6th graders report having done this)
2. riding with a drunk driver (31 percent)
3. gambling (31 percent)
4. threatening to physically harm someone (27 percent)
5. participating in group fighting (27 percent)

Table 3

child hit another child or yell, we need to get involved and teach more appropriate ways to act.

You'll find more examples of Search Institute's research on 6th graders throughout this book. While this isn't the same as having research on younger children, it brings up important questions we might not ask otherwise. For example, why is the most common asset for 6th graders Asset 15: Positive Peer Influence? Eighty-two percent of 6th graders report having this asset. And why do only 23 percent of 6th graders report having Asset 17: Creative Activities? As asset builders, we need to think about these questions and what they mean—not only to adolescents, but to the younger children in our care.

THE ASSETS DEFINED

In *What Young Children Need to Succeed,* each of the 40 developmental assets has its own chapter. Each chapter begins with a general definition of the asset, followed by specific definitions for four age groups: **infants** (birth to 12 months), **toddlers** (13 to 35 months), **preschoolers** (ages 3 to 5), and **elementary-age children** (ages 6 to 11).

You'll see these definitions as you read the chapters and start building assets with young children. We're also including the definitions in the next few pages so you can get an overview of how all 40 assets are defined for each age group.

You might look first at the general asset names on pages 14–15. Then turn to the definitions most relevant to your situation. For example, if you're the parent of an infant, see pages 16–17. The definitions for toddlers are on pages 18–19, the definitions for preschoolers are on pages 20–21, and the definitions for elementary-age children are on pages 22–23.

We invite you to copy these definitions to carry with you as reminders of your role as an asset builder. Or post them on your refrigerator, a bulletin board, or wherever you'll see them often.

40 Assets ALL Young Children Need to Succeed

Support

1. Family Support
2. Positive Family Communication
3. Other Adult Relationships
4. Caring Neighborhood
5. Caring Out-of-Home Climate
6. Parent Involvement in Out-of-Home Situations

Empowerment

7. Community Values Children
8. Children Are Given Useful Roles
9. Service to Others
10. Safety

Boundaries and Expectations

11. Family Boundaries
12. Out-of-Home Boundaries
13. Neighborhood Boundaries
14. Adult Role Models
15. Positive Peer Interaction and Influence
16. Appropriate Expectations for Growth

Constructive Use of Time

17. Creative Activities
18. Out-of-Home Activities
19. Religious Community
20. Positive, Supervised Time at Home

40 Assets ALL Young Children Need to Succeed (continued)

Commitment to Learning

21. Achievement Expectation and Motivation
22. Children Are Engaged in Learning
23. Stimulating Activity and Homework
24. Enjoyment of Learning and Bonding to School
25. Reading for Pleasure

Positive Values

26. Family Values Caring
27. Family Values Equality and Social Justice
28. Family Values Integrity
29. Family Values Honesty
30. Family Values Responsibility
31. Family Values Healthy Lifestyle

Social Competencies

32. Planning and Decision Making
33. Interpersonal Skills
34. Cultural Competence

35. Resistance Skills
36. Peaceful Conflict Resolution

Positive Identity

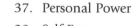

37. Personal Power
38. Self-Esteem
39. Sense of Purpose
40. Positive View of Personal Future

40 Assets INFANTS Need to Succeed
(Birth to 12 Months)

1. Family Support. Family life provides high levels of love and support.

2. Positive Family Communication. Parents communicate with infants in positive ways. Parents respond immediately to infants and respect their needs.

3. Other Adult Relationships. Parents have support from three or more adults and ask for help when needed. Children receive additional love and comfort from at least one adult other than their parents.

4. Caring Neighborhood. Children experience caring neighbors.

5. Caring Out-of-Home Climate. Children are in caring, encouraging environments outside the home.

6. Parent Involvement in Out-of-Home Situations. Parents are actively involved in communicating infants' needs to caretakers and others in situations outside the home.

7. Community Values Children. The family places infants at the center of family life. Other adults in the community value and appreciate infants.

8. Children Are Given Useful Roles. The family involves infants in family life.

9. Service to Others. Parents serve others in the community.

10. Safety. Children have safe environments at home, in out-of-home settings, and in the neighborhood. This includes childproofing these environments.

11. Family Boundaries. Parents are aware of infants' preferences and adapt the environment and schedule to suit infants' needs. Parents begin setting limits as infants become mobile.

12. Out-of-Home Boundaries. Childcare settings and other out-of-home environments have clear rules and consequences for older infants and consistently provide all infants with appropriate stimulation and enough rest.

13. Neighborhood Boundaries. Neighbors take responsibility for monitoring and supervising children's behavior as they begin to play and interact outside the home.

14. Adult Role Models. Parents and other adults model positive, responsible behavior.

15. Positive Peer Interaction and Influence. Infants observe siblings and other children interacting in positive ways. They have opportunities to interact with children of various ages.

16. Appropriate Expectations for Growth. Parents have realistic expectations for children's development at this age. Parents encourage development without pushing children beyond their own pace.

17. Creative Activities. Parents expose infants to music, art, or other creative aspects of the environment each day.

18. Out-of-Home Activities. Parents expose children to limited but stimulating situations outside the home. The family keeps children's needs in mind when attending events.

19. Religious Community. The family regularly attends religious programs or services while keeping children's needs in mind.

20. Positive, Supervised Time at Home. Parents supervise children at all times and provide predictable, enjoyable routines at home.

21. Achievement Expectation and Motivation. Family members are motivated to do well at work, at school, and in the community, and model their motivation for children.

22. Children Are Engaged in Learning. Parents and family members model responsive and attentive attitudes at work, at school, in the community, and at home.

From *What Young Children Need to Succeed* by Jolene L. Roehlkepartain and Nancy Leffert, Ph.D., © 2000 by Jolene L. Roehlkepartain and Search Institute. This page may be photocopied for personal use only. Free Spirit Publishing Inc., Minneapolis, MN; 800/735-7323; *www.freespirit.com.*

40 Assets INFANTS Need to Succeed (continued)

23. Stimulating Activity and Homework. Parents encourage children to explore and provide stimulating toys that match children's emerging skills. Parents are sensitive to children's dispositions, preferences, and level of development.

24. Enjoyment of Learning and Bonding to School. Parents enjoy learning and model this through their own learning activities.

25. Reading for Pleasure. Parents read to infants in enjoyable ways every day.

26. Family Values Caring. Parents convey their beliefs about helping others by modeling their helping behaviors.

27. Family Values Equality and Social Justice. Parents place a high value on promoting social equality, religious tolerance, and reducing hunger and poverty while modeling these beliefs for children.

28. Family Values Integrity. Parents act on their convictions, stand up for their beliefs, and communicate and model this in the family.

29. Family Values Honesty. Parents tell the truth and convey their belief in honesty through their actions.

30. Family Values Responsibility. Parents accept and take personal responsibility.

31. Family Values Healthy Lifestyle. Parents love children, setting the foundation for infants to develop healthy attitudes and beliefs about relationships. Parents model, monitor, and teach the importance of good health habits, and provide good nutritional choices and adequate rest and playtime.

32. Planning and Decision Making. Parents make all safety and care decisions for children and model safe behavior. As children become more independently mobile, parents allow them to make simple choices.

33. Interpersonal Skills. Parents model positive, constructive interactions with other people. Parents accept and are responsive to how infants express their feelings, seeing those expressions as cues to infants' needs.

34. Cultural Competence. Parents know and are comfortable with people of different cultural, racial, and/or ethnic backgrounds, and model this to children.

35. Resistance Skills. Parents model resistance skills through their own behavior

36. Peaceful Conflict Resolution. Parents behave in acceptable, nonviolent ways and assist children in developing these skills by helping them solve problems when they're faced with challenging or frustrating circumstances.

37. Personal Power. Parents feel they have control over things that happen in their own lives and model coping skills, demonstrating healthy ways to deal with frustrations and challenges. Parents respond to children so children begin to learn that they have influence over their immediate surroundings.

38. Self-Esteem. Parents create an environment where children can develop positive self-esteem, giving children appropriate, positive feedback and reinforcement about their skills and competencies.

39. Sense of Purpose. Parents report that their lives have purpose and demonstrate these beliefs through their behaviors. Infants are curious about the world around them.

40. Positive View of Personal Future. Parents are hopeful and positive about their personal future and work to provide a positive future for children.

40 Assets TODDLERS Need to Succeed
(Ages 13 to 35 Months)

1. Family Support. Family life provides high levels of love and support.

2. Positive Family Communication. Parents communicate with toddlers in positive ways. Parents respond to toddlers in a reasonable amount of time and respect their needs.

3. Other Adult Relationships. Parents have support from three or more adults and ask for help when needed. Children receive additional love and comfort from at least one adult other than their parents.

4. Caring Neighborhood. Children experience caring neighbors.

5. Caring Out-of-Home Climate. Children are in caring, encouraging environments outside the home.

6. Parent Involvement in Out-of-Home Situations. Parents are actively involved in helping toddlers succeed in situations outside the home. Parents communicate toddlers' needs to caretakers outside the home.

7. Community Values Children. The family places toddlers at the center of family life and recognizes the need to set limits for toddlers. Other adults in the community value and appreciate toddlers.

8. Children Are Given Useful Roles. The family involves toddlers in family life.

9. Service to Others. Parents serve others in the community.

10. Safety. Children have safe environments at home, in out-of-home settings, and in the neighborhood. This includes childproofing these environments.

11. Family Boundaries. Parents are aware of toddlers' preferences and adapt the environment to suit toddlers' needs. Parents set age-appropriate limits for toddlers.

12. Out-of-Home Boundaries. Childcare settings and other out-of-home environments have clear rules and consequences to protect toddlers while consistently providing appropriate stimulation and enough rest.

13. Neighborhood Boundaries. Neighbors take responsibility for monitoring and supervising children's behavior as they begin to play and interact outside the home.

14. Adult Role Models. Parents and other adults model positive, responsible behavior.

15. Positive Peer Interaction and Influence. Toddlers observe siblings and other children interacting in positive ways. They have opportunities to interact with children of various ages.

16. Appropriate Expectations for Growth. Parents have realistic expectations for children's development at this age. Parents encourage development without pushing children beyond their own pace.

17. Creative Activities. Parents expose toddlers to music, art, or other creative age-appropriate activities each day.

18. Out-of-Home Activities. Parents expose children to limited but stimulating situations outside the home. The family keeps children's needs in mind when attending events.

19. Religious Community. The family regularly attends religious programs or services while keeping children's needs in mind.

20. Positive, Supervised Time at Home. Parents supervise children at all times and provide predictable, enjoyable routines at home.

21. Achievement Expectation and Motivation. Family members are motivated to do well at work, at school, and in the community, and model their motivation for children.

22. Children Are Engaged in Learning. Parents and family members model responsive and attentive attitudes at work, at school, in the community, and at home.

From *What Young Children Need to Succeed* by Jolene L. Roehlkepartain and Nancy Leffert, Ph.D., © 2000 by Jolene L. Roehlkepartain and Search Institute. This page may be photocopied for personal use only. Free Spirit Publishing Inc., Minneapolis, MN; 800/735-7323; *www.freespirit.com*.

40 Assets TODDLERS Need to Succeed (continued)

23. Stimulating Activity and Homework. Parents encourage children to explore and provide stimulating toys that match children's emerging skills. Parents are sensitive to children's dispositions, preferences, and level of development.

24. Enjoyment of Learning and Bonding to School. Parents enjoy learning and express this through their own learning activities.

25. Reading for Pleasure. Parents read to toddlers every day and find ways for toddlers to participate in enjoyable reading experiences.

26. Family Values Caring. Parents convey their beliefs about helping others by modeling their helping behaviors.

27. Family Values Equality and Social Justice. Parents place a high value on promoting social equality, religious tolerance, and reducing hunger and poverty while modeling these beliefs for children.

28. Family Values Integrity. Parents act on their convictions, stand up for their beliefs, and communicate and model this in the family.

29. Family Values Honesty. Parents tell the truth and convey their belief in honesty through their actions.

30. Family Values Responsibility. Parents accept and take personal responsibility.

31. Family Values Healthy Lifestyle. Parents love children, setting the foundation for toddlers to develop healthy attitudes and beliefs about relationships. Parents model, monitor, and teach the importance of good health habits, and provide good nutritional choices and adequate rest and playtime.

32. Planning and Decision Making. Parents make all safety and care decisions for children and model safe behavior. As children become more independently mobile, parents allow them to make simple choices.

33. Interpersonal Skills. Parents model positive, constructive interactions with other people. Parents accept and are responsive to how toddlers use actions and words to express their feelings, seeing those expressions as cues to toddlers' needs.

34. Cultural Competence. Parents know and are comfortable with people of different cultural, racial, and/or ethnic backgrounds, and model this to children.

35. Resistance Skills. Parents model resistance skills through their own behavior. Parents aren't overwhelmed by toddlers' needs and demonstrate appropriate resistance skills.

36. Peaceful Conflict Resolution. Parents behave in acceptable, nonviolent ways and assist children in developing these skills by helping them solve problems when they're faced with challenging or frustrating circumstances.

37. Personal Power. Parents feel they have control over things that happen in their own lives and model coping skills, demonstrating healthy ways to deal with frustrations and challenges. Parents respond to children so children begin to learn that they have influence over their immediate surroundings.

38. Self-Esteem. Parents create an environment where children can develop positive self-esteem, giving children appropriate, positive feedback and reinforcement about their skills and competencies.

39. Sense of Purpose. Parents report that their lives have purpose and model these beliefs through their behaviors. Children are curious and explore the world around them.

40. Positive View of Personal Future. Parents are hopeful and positive about their personal future and work to provide a positive future for children.

From *What Young Children Need to Succeed* by Jolene L. Roehlkepartain and Nancy Leffert, Ph.D., © 2000 by Jolene L. Roehlkepartain and Search Institute. This page may be photocopied for personal use only; Free Spirit Publishing Inc., Minneapolis, MN; 800/735-7323; *www.freespirit.com.*

40 Assets PRESCHOOLERS Need to Succeed
(Ages 3 to 5 Years)

1. Family Support. Family life provides high levels of love and support.

2. Positive Family Communication. Parents and preschoolers communicate positively. Preschoolers seek out parents for help with difficult tasks or situations.

3. Other Adult Relationships. Preschoolers have support from at least one adult other than their parents. Their parents have support from people outside the home.

4. Caring Neighborhood. Children experience caring neighbors.

5. Caring Out-of-Home Climate. Children are in caring, encouraging environments outside the home.

6. Parent Involvement in Out-of-Home Situations. Parents are actively involved in helping preschoolers succeed in situations outside the home. Parents communicate preschoolers' needs to caretakers outside the home.

7. Community Values Children. Parents and other adults in the community value and appreciate preschoolers.

8. Children Are Given Useful Roles. Parents and other adults create ways preschoolers can help out and gradually include preschoolers in age-appropriate tasks.

9. Service to Others. The family serves others in the community together.

10. Safety. Preschoolers have safe environments at home, in out-of-home settings, and in the neighborhood. This includes childproofing these environments.

11. Family Boundaries. The family has clear rules and consequences. The family monitors preschoolers and consistently demonstrates appropriate behavior through modeling and limit setting.

12. Out-of-Home Boundaries. Childcare settings and other out-of-home environments have clear rules and consequences to protect preschoolers while consistently providing appropriate stimulation and enough rest.

13. Neighborhood Boundaries. Neighbors take responsibility for monitoring and supervising children's behavior as they begin to play and interact outside the home.

14. Adult Role Models. Parents and other adults model positive, responsible behavior.

15. Positive Peer Interaction and Influence. Preschoolers are encouraged to play and interact with other children in safe, well-supervised settings.

16. Appropriate Expectations for Growth. Adults have realistic expectations for children's development at this age. Parents, caregivers, and other adults encourage children to achieve and develop their unique talents.

17. Creative Activities. Preschoolers participate in music, art, dramatic play, or other creative activities each day.

18. Out-of-Home Activities. Preschoolers interact in stimulating ways with children outside the family. The family keeps preschoolers' needs in mind when attending events.

19. Religious Community. The family regularly attends religious programs or services while keeping children's needs in mind.

20. Positive, Supervised Time at Home. Preschoolers are supervised by an adult at all times. Preschoolers spend most evenings and weekends at home with their parents in predictable, enjoyable routines.

21. Achievement Expectation and Motivation. Parents and other adults convey and reinforce expectations to do well at work, at school, in the community, and within the family.

22. Children Are Engaged in Learning. Parents and family

From *What Young Children Need to Succeed* by Jolene L. Roehlkepartain and Nancy Leffert, Ph.D., © 2000 by Jolene L. Roehlkepartain and Search Institute. This page may be photocopied for personal use only. Free Spirit Publishing Inc., Minneapolis, MN; 800/735-7323; *www.freespirit.com*.

40 Assets PRESCHOOLERS Need to Succeed (continued)

members model responsive and attentive attitudes at work, at school, in the community, and at home.

23. Stimulating Activity and Homework. Parents encourage children to explore and provide stimulating toys that match children's emerging skills. Parents are sensitive to children's dispositions, preferences, and level of development.

24. Enjoyment of Learning and Bonding to School. Parents and other adults enjoy learning and engage preschoolers in learning activities.

25. Reading for Pleasure. Adults read to preschoolers for at least 30 minutes over the course of a day, encouraging preschoolers to participate.

26. Family Values Caring. Preschoolers are encouraged to express sympathy for someone who is distressed and begin to develop a variety of helping behaviors.

27. Family Values Equality and Social Justice. Parents place a high value on promoting social equality, religious tolerance, and reducing hunger and poverty while modeling these beliefs for children.

28. Family Values Integrity. Parents act on their convictions, stand up for their beliefs, and communicate and model this in the family.

29. Family Values Honesty. Preschoolers learn the difference between telling the truth and lying.

30. Family Values Responsibility. Preschoolers learn that their actions affect other people.

31. Family Values Healthy Lifestyle. Parents and other adults model, monitor, and teach the importance of good health habits. Preschoolers begin to learn healthy sexual attitudes and beliefs as well as respect for others.

32. Planning and Decision Making. Preschoolers begin to make simple choices, solve simple

problems, and develop simple plans at age-appropriate levels.

33. Interpersonal Skills. Preschoolers play and interact with other children and adults. They freely express their feelings and learn to put their feelings into words. Parents and other adults model and teach empathy

34. Cultural Competence. Preschoolers are exposed in positive ways to information about and to people of different cultural, racial, and/or ethnic backgrounds

35. Resistance Skills. Preschoolers are taught to resist participating in inappropriate or dangerous behavior.

36. Peaceful Conflict Resolution. Parents and other adults model positive ways to resolve conflicts. Preschoolers are taught and begin to practice nonviolent, acceptable ways to deal with challenging and frustrating situations.

37. Personal Power. Parents feel they have control over things that happen in their own lives and model coping skills, demonstrating healthy ways to deal with frustrations and challenges. Parents respond to children so children begin to learn that they have influence over their immediate surroundings.

38. Self-Esteem. Parents create an environment where children can develop positive self-esteem, giving children appropriate, positive feedback and reinforcement about their skills and competencies.

39. Sense of Purpose. Parents report that their lives have purpose and model these beliefs through their behaviors. Children are curious and explore the world around them.

40. Positive View of Personal Future. Parents are hopeful and positive about their personal future and work to provide a positive future for children.

From *What Young Children Need to Succeed* by Jolene L. Roehlkepartain and Nancy Leffert, Ph.D., © 2000 by Jolene L. Roehlkepartain and Search Institute. This page may be photocopied for personal use only. Free Spirit Publishing Inc., Minneapolis, MN; 800/735-7323; *www.freespirit.com.*

40 Assets ELEMENTARY-AGE CHILDREN Need to Succeed
(Ages 6 to 11 Years)

1. Family Support. Family life provides high levels of love and support.

2. Positive Family Communication. Parents and children communicate positively. Children are willing to seek advice and counsel from their parents.

3. Other Adult Relationships. Children have support from adults other than their parents.

4. Caring Neighborhood. Children experience caring neighbors.

5. Caring Out-of-Home Climate. School and other activities provide caring, encouraging environments for children.

6. Parent Involvement in Out-of-Home Situations. Parents are actively involved in helping children succeed in school and in other situations outside the home.

7. Community Values Children. Children feel that the family and community value and appreciate children.

8. Children Are Given Useful Roles. Children are included in age-appropriate family tasks and decisions and are given useful roles at home and in the community.

9. Service to Others. Children serve others in the community with their family or in other settings.

10. Safety. Children are safe at home, at school, and in the neighborhood.

11. Family Boundaries. The family has clear rules and consequences and monitors children's activities and whereabouts.

12. Out-of-Home Boundaries. Schools and other out-of-home environments provide clear rules and consequences.

13. Neighborhood Boundaries. Neighbors take responsibility for monitoring children's behavior.

14. Adult Role Models. Parents and other adults model positive, responsible behavior.

15. Positive Peer Interaction and Influence. Children interact with other children who model responsible behavior and have opportunities to play and interact in safe, well-supervised settings.

16. Appropriate Expectations for Growth. Adults have realistic expectations for children's development at this age. Parents, caregivers, and other adults encourage children to achieve and develop their unique talents.

17. Creative Activities. Children participate in music, art, drama, or other creative activities for at least three hours a week at home and elsewhere.

18. Out-of-Home Activities. Children spend one hour or more each week in extracurricular school activities or structured community programs.

19. Religious Community. The family attends religious programs or services for at least one hour per week.

20. Positive, Supervised Time at Home. Children spend most evenings and weekends at home with their parents in predictable, enjoyable routines.

21. Achievement Expectation and Motivation. Children are motivated to do well in school and other activities.

From *What Young Children Need to Succeed* by Jolene L. Roehlkepartain and Nancy Leffert, Ph.D., © 2000 by Jolene L. Roehlkepartain and Search Institute. This page may be photocopied for personal use only. Free Spirit Publishing Inc., Minneapolis, MN; 800/735-7323; *www.freespirit.com*.

40 Assets ELEMENTARY-AGE CHILDREN Need to Succeed *(continued)*

22. Children Are Engaged in Learning. Children are responsive, attentive, and actively engaged in learning.

23. Stimulating Activity and Homework. Parents and teachers encourage children to explore and engage in stimulating activities. Children do homework when it's assigned.

24. Enjoyment of Learning and Bonding to School. Children enjoy learning and care about their school.

25. Reading for Pleasure. Children and an adult read together for at least 30 minutes a day. Children also enjoy reading or looking at books or magazines on their own.

26. Family Values Caring. Children are encouraged to help other people.

27. Family Values Equality and Social Justice. Children begin to show interest in making the community a better place.

28. Family Values Integrity. Children begin to act on their convictions and stand up for their beliefs.

29. Family Values Honesty. Children begin to value honesty and act accordingly.

30. Family Values Responsibility. Children begin to accept and take personal responsibility for age-appropriate tasks.

31. Family Values Healthy Lifestyle. Children begin to value good health habits and learn healthy sexual attitudes and beliefs as well as respect for others.

32. Planning and Decision Making. Children begin to learn how to plan ahead and

make choices at appropriate developmental levels.

33. Interpersonal Skills. Children interact with adults and children and can make friends. Children express and articulate feelings in appropriate ways and empathize with others.

34. Cultural Competence. Children know about and are comfortable with people of different cultural, racial, and/or ethnic backgrounds.

35. Resistance Skills. Children start developing the ability to resist negative peer pressure and dangerous situations.

36. Peaceful Conflict Resolution. Children try to resolve conflicts nonviolently.

37. Personal Power. Children begin to feel they have control over things that happen to them. They begin to manage

frustrations and challenges in ways that have positive results for themselves and others.

38. Self-Esteem. Children report having high self-esteem.

39. Sense of Purpose. Children report that their lives have purpose and actively engage their skills.

40. Positive View of Personal Future. Children are hopeful and positive about their personal future.

From *What Young Children Need to Succeed* by Jolene L. Roehlkepartain and Nancy Leffert, Ph.D., © 2000 by Jolene L. Roehlkepartain and Search Institute. This page may be photocopied for personal use only. Free Spirit Publishing Inc., Minneapolis, MN; 800/735-7323; *www.freespirit.com*.

BUILDING
THE ASSETS

THE SUPPORT ASSETS

To grow and thrive, children need supportive adults and supportive environments. Anyone who spends time with children can
love, care for, encourage, and affirm them. This support can
happen anywhere, at any time.

The support category includes six developmental assets for children from birth through age 11:

The Support Assets

Asset 1: Family Support

Asset 2: Positive Family Communication

Asset 3: Other Adult Relationships

Asset 4: Caring Neighborhood

Asset 5: Caring Out-of-Home Climate

Asset 6: Parent Involvement in Out-of-Home Situations

When Search Institute surveyed 6th graders, they found that children experience some of the support assets more than others. Here are the percentages of these children who reported each of the assets in their lives:*

Asset 1: Family Support   **79%**

Asset 2: Positive Family Communication   **40%**

Asset 3: Other Adult Relationships   **41%**

Asset 4: Caring Neighborhood   **50%**

Asset 5: Caring School Climate   **38%**

Asset 6: Parent Involvement in Schooling **44%**

---

*Some of the asset names in the survey of 6th graders are different from those relating to younger children. The survey's asset names are the names that apply to older children and teens. The asset names in *What Young Children Need to Succeed* take into account developmental and situational differences of young children. See pages 3–5 for further information about asset language.

Asset 1

FAMILY SUPPORT

**Children need love, comfort, encouragement,
and support from their families.
Parents are consistent and positive
while responding to children's needs.**

How Search Institute defines this asset . . .

For infants, toddlers, preschoolers, and elementary-age children: Family life provides high levels of love and support.

ALL CHILDREN

- Smile at children and their parents, too, to show your support.
- Learn the names of children you often see. Greet them by name and say hello.
- Get close to children. Kneel down, squat, or sit on the floor when you spend time with them.

INFANTS

- Share the excitement when a child is born. Give a gift or a card. Celebrate!
- Hold infants and talk to them during feedings.

- Help new parents. Ask if you can run an errand for them, or offer to baby-sit so parents can have a night out.
- Marvel at how babies grow. Cheer on their developments.

TODDLERS

- Praise toddlers as they master new skills, such as walking down the stairs while holding the railing. Comfort them when they're frustrated.
- Offer to watch a toddler (or to stop by when the child naps) to give parents a break.
- Say "yes" to toddlers more often than you say "no." Praise them often and enthusiastically.
- Have fun with toddlers. Play simple games that make them laugh, such as hiding toys for them to find.

PRESCHOOLERS

- When you meet a preschooler, ask her how old she is. Chat with her about her day, an upcoming holiday, or her visit to the zoo.
- Many preschoolers like stickers. Carry stickers with you and give some to preschoolers you meet.

 DID YOU KNOW?

Strong connections build more confident children. According to researchers at the University of Minnesota, children who form strong bonds with warm, responsive caregivers cope with difficult times more easily than children who don't have this connection. Supported children are also more curious, get along better with other children, and perform better in school.

Source: *The First Years Last Forever* (Beverly Hills, CA: I Am Your Child Campaign, The Reiner Foundation, 1997).

- Introduce a preschooler to new situations to expand his mind. You might show him many different colors and sizes of seeds or take him to a museum and look at artwork together.
- Let preschoolers choose a game or activity, then play it with them.
- Share a preschooler's excitement about her interests: ants on the sidewalk, airplanes in the air, silly noises she can make, and goofy songs she knows.
- When a preschooler invites you to a tea party or puppet show, say, "Thank you for asking me. I'd love to come." Sip invisible tea or laugh at the funny things the puppets do. Tell the preschooler how much you enjoy spending time with him.

RESOURCE

Wonderful Ways to Love a Child by Judy Ford (Berkeley: Fine Communications, 1997) gives inspiring, practical ideas on supporting children.

ELEMENTARY-AGE CHILDREN

- Have fun with sidewalk chalk. Write a sidewalk message to a child on the first day of school—or anytime.
- Attend a neighborhood child's school program, recital, concert, or sports event.
- Follow children's passions and interests, even those that seem unusual or outlandish. If a child likes dinosaurs, learn about the allosaurus and the deinonychus. If clowns fascinate her, take her to the circus or register her for a clown camp.
- Answer a child's questions. If you're stumped, admit it. Find out the answer and tell the child what you've learned, or discover the answer together.
- When you and a child disagree, be respectful and let him know you still care. Say, "It's okay for us to have different opinions. Thank you for letting me know what you think."
- Ask children about their collections. Watch for interesting stamps, rocks, international coins, stickers, baseball cards,

books, and other things children collect. Talk about the things you collect, too.

- Spend time with a child, doing things that are fun for her. If she likes soccer, for example, offer to practice with her.

Asset 2

POSITIVE FAMILY COMMUNICATION

Parents communicate with children in positive ways and respect and respond to their needs. As children learn to talk, they are comfortable asking their parents for help and advice.

How Search Institute defines this asset . . .

For infants: Parents communicate with infants in positive ways. Parents respond immediately to infants and respect their needs.

For toddlers: Parents communicate with toddlers in positive ways. Parents respond to toddlers in a reasonable amount of time and respect their needs.

For preschoolers: Parents and preschoolers communicate positively. Preschoolers seek out parents for help with difficult tasks or situations.

For elementary-age children: Parents and children communicate positively. Children are willing to seek advice and counsel from their parents.

ALL CHILDREN

- Look at children when you speak to them. Eye contact is a simple way to let them know you care.
- When a child is upset, be sympathetic. Ask, "Can you tell me what's wrong?" Do what you can to meet the child's needs.

- Positive communication can happen without words. Snuggling or putting your arm around a child says a lot.
- Learn what tickles a child's funnybone. Some children like silly games and crazy faces, while others like knock-knock jokes and riddles. Do fun things and laugh together.

RESOURCE

Riddles in a Jar® by Deborah Stein (Minneapolis: Attitude Matters, Inc., 1999) has a year's supply of wacky, puzzling riddles printed on slips of paper. Children can select a riddle each day from the jar.

INFANTS

- Rock infants often. Rock in a rocking chair. Rock while you're standing and holding the child. Gentle motion makes a child feel comfortable and cared for.
- Make conversations with an infant upbeat. A baby can detect your mood, even though he can't understand the words. Speak naturally. Avoid using "baby talk." The infant is learning from listening to you, so he needs to hear correct language.

 DID YOU KNOW?

Physical touch is the positive family communication that infants need most. Touch, in the form of infant massage, has been shown to benefit premature infants. Researcher Tiffany Field found that preterm infants (those born early) who were massaged gained more weight and performed developmental tasks better than preterm infants who weren't massaged.

Source: Tiffany M. Field, "Touch Therapies Across the Life Span," in *Handbook of Diversity Issues in Health Psychology,* edited by Pamela M. Kato and Traci Mann (New York: Plenum, 1996), 46–97.

- Sing to an infant. (Babies don't care if you're off-key!) Sing along with the radio or a recording.
- Talk to infants during routine activities. Simple, specific adult language will help the child develop language skills. For example, say, "Look at how your toes wiggle" when changing a diaper. Or say, "Yum! You love squash!" when feeding the baby food she likes.
- Infants communicate by crying. Respond to this right away. They may be hungry, tired, or wet. They may need you to hold and soothe them. Responding quickly tells babies that you're there to support them.

TODDLERS

- Play "show me" with a toddler. Ask a toddler to bring you his favorite book, a toy, or something to play with together. Toddlers like finding things to bring to an adult.
- Praise a child when she says, "Look what I did!" Be proud of her accomplishments and encourage her to do more. For example, what may look like scribbles on paper could be a great masterpiece to a toddler. Say, "Look at how creative you are! Isn't drawing fun?"
- Stay positive when setting limits for toddlers. Tell a toddler how to act as well as how not to act. For example, say, "Don't throw the toy. Give it to me gently, like this." (For more on setting limits, see Asset 11: Family Boundaries, pages 91–96.)
- Physically touch toddlers often, but respect their feelings when they don't want to be touched. Toddlers want to have distance sometimes. Don't take this as a sign that a toddler doesn't need you. Try again later—or when the toddler asks to be held.
- Answer toddlers' questions. When toddlers ask, "What's that?" give a simple reply, such as, "It's a bird." Be patient with the many questions they ask. Remember that this is the way toddlers learn about the world. It's also their way of having conversations with you.

Preschoolers

- Make talking a part of the bedtime routine. Some families read a bedtime story together. Others talk quietly for a few minutes after turning off the lights. Preschoolers like the routine of bedtime rituals.

- Delight in preschoolers' "Why?" questions. If you don't know an answer, say so and find out together.

- Watch the balance of conversations. Everyone (both children and adults) should have the chance to talk—and listen. Let preschoolers start conversations sometimes.

- Help preschoolers when they ask you to. If you're busy (with a phone conversation, for example), be clear about who else can help him now or when you can help him later.

- Ask questions such as, "What's your favorite food?" or "What's your favorite toy?" Preschoolers love answering questions.

- Help preschoolers put their feelings into words. For example, you might say, "When something like that happens to me, I feel sad. How do you feel?"

Elementary-Age Children

- Vary how you greet an elementary-age child. Don't always ask, "How was your day?" Instead, say, "Hey, it's great to see you. I'm glad you're here."

- Children prefer different types of physical contact—be sensitive to this. Some like having their backs rubbed. Some like holding a parent's hand for part of a walk. Others enjoy playful wrestling or a friendly football game.

- Ask questions when children say "Did you know . . ." and tell you things they've learned. Engage children in conversation.

- Make mealtime talking time. You might have each person take a turn saying something about a specific topic or about his or her day. Possible topics: "If you had a million dollars to give away, who would you give it to and why?" "If you could choose any place in the world to visit, where would you go and why?"

- Ask questions that help children get (and stay) in touch with their feelings. For example, ask, "What makes you sad? happy? disappointed? angry? confused?" Talk about feelings and share some of your ideas for dealing with those feelings.
- What are children interested in? Find out. Talk with them about the solar system, math tricks, a children's author, a sports hero, or current events. Ask them to find out an interesting fact to surprise you with next time you talk.

Asset 3

OTHER ADULT RELATIONSHIPS

All children receive love and comfort from at least one adult other than their parents. Parents have support from individuals outside the home.

How Search Institute defines this asset . . .

For infants and toddlers: Parents have support from three or more adults and ask for help when needed. Children receive additional love and comfort from at least one adult other than their parents.

For preschoolers: Preschoolers have support from at least one adult other than their parents. Their parents have support from people outside the home.

For elementary-age children: Children have support from adults other than their parents.

ALL CHILDREN

- Adults can support both a child and his parents. Parents need care and assistance just like everyone else.
- Look children in the eye when you meet them. Say hello, call them by name, and share a warm smile.
- Volunteer at a school, preschool, childcare setting, or religious education class. Reading a couple of books or playing games can make a difference.

INFANTS

- Be warm, responsive, and sensitive when you're around an infant. Do things that make the infant smile.
- Find ways to help new parents. Offer to run errands or to baby-sit while parents take a break.
- Give infants space when they need it. Be sensitive to their cues. Constant attention, even from caring adults, will make babies tired. But be close to infants when they want closeness.

TODDLERS

- Examine your attitudes about toddlers. Many adults are afraid of toddlers because they've heard so much about the "terrible twos." Toddlers can have difficult moments, but they are also endearing.

RESOURCE

Making the "Terrible" Twos Terrific! by John Rosemond (Kansas City, MO: Andrews McMeel Publishing, 1993) discusses the importance of understanding the needs of parents and children during this challenging time in child development.

- Be sensitive to a toddler's moods—she may be warm and cuddly one moment and distracted and distant the next. Don't take these mood changes personally or think the toddler is being "bad." This is just the way toddlers behave.
- Read a toddler's face for cues about how to act. Keep doing things that make him light up and smile. Change what you're doing when he frowns or pulls away.
- Help an exasperated parent of a toddler who's acting up in public. Distract the toddler to help her calm down.

PRESCHOOLERS

- When you visit families who have preschoolers, spend time with the children as well as the adults. Ask preschoolers what they like to play.
- Look for simple ways to have fun with preschoolers. Eat popsicles together. Blow some bubbles.
- Have a crazy hair day. Let a preschooler give you a wild hairdo, then give the preschooler one, too. Both girls and boys love this. Use water, combs, bobby pins, barrettes, beads, clips, and ponytail holders.
- Send a birthday card with stickers on a preschooler's birthday. Or leave a birthday message on the answering machine.

ELEMENTARY-AGE CHILDREN

- Create a riddle or knock-knock joke ritual with a child. Have the child tell you a joke, then share one of your own.
- Be silly with a child. Make faces. Show your best tricks: Can you roll your tongue? stand on your head? Ask the child to show you his amazing feats.
- Make a stronger connection with children you know. Intentionally build an ongoing relationship with a child you like. Construct a model ship together or help her with a science project.
- Send postcards to children when you're traveling.
- Find out about a child's interests. Clip and send newspaper photos and articles about the child's favorite athlete. When you're on a walk, look for rocks to add to a child's rock collection.
- Attend a child's sports event, play, concert, or another activity. Afterward, go out of your way to congratulate the child and let him know you were there.

ASSETS IN ACTION
Supporting Neighborhood Children

All the neighborhood children know where Gary and Carrie Surber live. The Surbers, who have a daughter, have made it known that their home is the gathering place for any child who wants to visit. Children run races, play games, or simply come to talk in the Surbers' backyard—or on the front porch. "It's front porch parenting," Carrie says. "You just hang out, spending lots of time with kids."

Asset 4

CARING NEIGHBORHOOD

Children have neighbors who care for and about them.

How Search Institute defines this asset . . .

For infants, toddlers, preschoolers, and elementary-age children: Children experience caring neighbors.

ALL CHILDREN

- Introduce yourself to a neighborhood family with children. Point out where you live. Say hello and chat for a few minutes when you see them.
- Treat children in your neighborhood with the same respect and courtesy you show adults. Expect them to treat other people respectfully, too.
- In the summer, hang out in the front yard (instead of the backyard) and greet adults and children who pass by. If you live in an apartment, spend some time in shared living spaces or at a nearby playground. If you live in the country, have a potluck and invite families with children.
- Create a neighborhood service project that children and adults can do together. Collect canned food for food shelves. Clean up a park. Offer to plant flowers, mow the lawn, or rake the leaves for a homebound neighbor.

RESOURCE

The Center for Neighborhood Technology
2125 West North Avenue
Chicago, IL 60647
Telephone: (773) 278-4800
Web site: *www.cnt.org/*

This organization publishes *The Neighborhood Works* magazine, which includes articles about creating effective, caring neighborhoods.

• Look around your neighborhood—is it a safe and caring place for children to learn and grow? Share any concerns with the neighborhood organization or city council.

INFANTS

• Bring a gift or greeting card to neighborhood parents who have a new baby.
• Ask parents of infants how they're doing with their new baby. Be supportive.
• When a baby is born, mark the date on your calendar. Send a note to the child—and the parents—on the child's first birthday.

TODDLERS

• Pick dandelion bouquets with a toddler and give them to the toddler's parents.
• Celebrate the first day of each new season by inviting a toddler outside to enjoy the snow, the rain, the butterflies, or the fallen leaves.
• Take a toddler on a neighborhood adventure. Ask him to name things he sees. Look for sunshine on skyscrapers. Be on the lookout for squirrels. Investigate a corn stalk.
• Invite a toddler and his parents to go for a walk. Offer to push the stroller.

- Go out of your way to talk to the toddlers you know in your neighborhood. Ask simple questions like "How many teeth do you have?" or "Do you have any fingers inside those mittens?"
- Play the animal guessing game with toddlers. Imitate different animal noises and have children guess which animal makes that sound.

PRESCHOOLERS

- Make a neighborhood treasure map for children. (Get permission from neighbors if you want to include their yards on the map.) Bury a surprise inside a sealed jar in a flower bed or garden, or hide it under the newspaper in front of an apartment door.
- Together, do crayon rubbings of objects you find in the neighborhood: leaves, imprints in concrete, and so on.
- Is your pet friendly with children? If so, introduce it to preschoolers who live in your neighborhood.
- Set up a free lemonade or juice stand. Give children a cool drink when they're playing outside on hot days.

ELEMENTARY-AGE CHILDREN

- Play "name that neighbor." Walk through the neighborhood together and name all the neighbors you can.
- Find out what neighborhood children like to do. Let children use your basketball hoop or play in your yard when you're around to supervise.
- Leave a message (hang a note on a door or write in chalk on a sidewalk) on the child's first day of school. Sign your name.
- Ask children in your neighborhood about their pets. Find out the pets' names and ask the children why they chose them.
- Join neighborhood children's football, kickball, basketball, or other games.

ASSETS IN ACTION
Creating Caring Neighborhoods

From May through Labor Day, neighborhoods in Findlay, Ohio, have an asset-building Neighborhood Porch Cookie Campaign. Someone in each participating neighborhood invites neighbors over to their porch, patio, deck, driveway, or yard to eat cookies and drink lemonade. Children and adults then spend time getting to know each other and building relationships. After one of these gatherings, a mother of two boys said, "It was fun, didn't cost much, and didn't take much time. I didn't even have to clean my house!"

Asset 5

CARING OUT-OF-HOME CLIMATE

Children spend time in encouraging, caring environments outside the home.

How Search Institute defines this asset . . .

For infants, toddlers, and preschoolers: Children are in caring, encouraging environments outside the home.

For elementary-age children: School and other activities provide caring, encouraging environments for children.

ALL CHILDREN

- Watch for signs of a caring environment: caregivers and children who enjoy learning and being together. Compliment the staff when you see these signs. Ask questions when you don't.
- Is the decor appropriate and safe for children? Make sure decorations are placed where children can see them.
- Get to know caregivers personally. Find out about their hobbies and interests.
- The facilities should be clean, in good repair, and free of vandalism. This helps children feel protected and secure. If the facility needs cleanup or repair, talk to staff and other adults. Together, find ways to make improvements.

- Children speak with their actions and body language as well as their words. Children who don't feel welcomed and cared for may not want to leave home. They'll act in inappropriate ways, and they may be moodier than usual. Talk to teachers or caregivers to help you find out what's wrong.

DID YOU KNOW?

For young children, an out-of-home environment is a childcare or educational program. Here are a few common types of childcare settings:

- Childcare centers usually provide care to several children at the same time. These centers can be publicly funded or privately owned, and may be part of a chain. Most states license these types of centers and require regular inspections.

- Family childcare settings operate from the childcare provider's home. In some cases, the caregiver is also caring for his or her own children. Some of these providers are licensed by the state, while others are not.

- In-home care is provided by a caregiver or nanny who comes to the child's home.

- Relative care is provided by an extended family member.

- Congregational nurseries may be licensed childcare centers run by religious organizations or less formal environments where parents can leave children while they attend religious services or events—or something in between.

- Preschools usually help children develop skills they'll need later in school. Most preschools are licensed.

For elementary-age children, school is the primary out-of-home environment. Other away-from-home settings include extracurricular activities and before- and after-school care.

RESOURCE

National Child Care Association
1016 Rosser Street
Conyers, GA 30012
Toll-free phone: 1-800-543-7161
Web site: *www.nccanet.org/*

The National Child Care Association (NCCA) is a professional trade association focusing on the needs of licensed, private child and education programs. The NCCA also helps parents looking for quality childcare by providing information about NCCA member centers across the country.

INFANTS

- Notice how caregivers interact with infants. Are they loving and caring? Do they meet infants' needs immediately?
- Monitor staff turnover at the childcare center. Too much (even with skilled caregivers) can cause stress for an infant.
- Tell childcare workers how much you appreciate what they do. Be specific. For example, you might say, "The baby loves being rocked to sleep. Thanks for doing that."
- Advocate for higher childcare standards in your state. Every year, *Working Mother* magazine publishes a state-by-state assessment of these standards in its July/August issue. To learn how your state rates, check the library or contact *Working Mother* magazine, P.O. Box 5240, Harlan, IA 51593; toll-free phone: 1-800-234-9675; Web site: *www.workingmother.com*.
- When you notice a childcare environment begin to slip (if caregivers act distant or stressed, for example), talk to a caregiver about your concerns. Don't wait for the situation to improve on its own.

TODDLERS

- Be happy when toddlers call their caregivers "Mom" or "Dad" and their parents by their caregivers' names. This shows that the toddler feels comfortable with the care she's getting.

- Make sure toddlers have their own cribs or cots, bedding, eating utensils, and comfort objects (such as a blanket, stuffed animal, or doll) at childcare settings.

- Drop in at a toddler's childcare center when you're not expected to see how caring the environment is.

- Toddlers thrive in open spaces, both indoors and out. Even in climates with cold winters, toddlers need to get outside. Make sure that childcare workers are willing to put the extra effort into bundling and unbundling toddlers so they can enjoy the outdoors.

PRESCHOOLERS

- Look for a variety of daily activities, including music, reading, outdoor play, indoor play, art projects, free time, and quiet time. Children thrive when they're both cared for and stimulated.

- Encourage caregivers to play with preschoolers individually as well as in a group.

- Contribute what you can to preschool learning centers. Many preschools could use costumes, shoes, and clothing for the dramatic play center, play food for the kitchen learning center, and other items. Ask how you can help.

ELEMENTARY-AGE CHILDREN

- Learn more about the importance of a caring school and discuss what you've learned with others. List attributes of a caring school (it's a place where teachers and administrators know and care for each other, it promotes creativity and learning, and so on). If you have any concerns, share them with a teacher or a school administrator.

- Find out how children feel about their school. Do they think it's a caring place? Why or why not? Ask them to use specific examples to explain their feelings.

- Recognize the thoughtful work teachers do. Thank the teacher throughout the year. On National Teacher Day, which is the first Tuesday of the first full week in May, send a thank-you card. Or, if you can afford it, treat the child's teacher to breakfast or dinner.

- Find out about your community's before- and after-school programs for children of working parents. Is the need being met? If not, talk with school officials and community leaders about developing appropriate programs. Offer help if you can.

- Learn the names of children and adults in the child's classroom and after-school clubs. Greeting people by name shows that you care.

- Have children plan ways to improve their school and after-school environments (they might suggest a fund-raising dinner, for example). Get children involved in the when, where, and how of the event, and help them decide what to do with the money that's raised.

 ## ASSETS IN ACTION
Supporting Caring Adults

Educator and parent Lynn Stambaugh of Englewood, Colorado, created a list of all the adults who frequently spent time with her kids—not just teachers, but also music instructors, bus drivers, coaches, custodians, and others. Then she wrote a letter to each of these people, saying, "As an adult working with young people, you play a very important role in the lives of our children." She described the developmental assets, highlighting the ones she thought each adult built. "You make a difference," she concluded. "Thank you for all your hard work and dedication."

Asset 6

PARENT INVOLVEMENT IN OUT-OF-HOME SITUATIONS

Parents talk about their children's needs with caregivers and teachers, and help their children succeed outside the home.

How Search Institute defines this asset . . .

For infants: Parents are actively involved in communicating infants' needs to caretakers and others in situations outside the home.

For toddlers and preschoolers: Parents are actively involved in helping toddlers and preschoolers succeed in situations outside the home. Parents communicate toddlers' and preschoolers' needs to caretakers outside the home.

For elementary-age children: Parents are actively involved in helping children succeed in school and in other situations outside the home.

ALL CHILDREN

- Keep in touch with the childcare director. Point out what you like and make concrete suggestions about ways to improve the environment. If you can, coordinate some people to paint a room, fix equipment, or do other tasks.
- If possible, support the fund-raisers of childcare centers and schools.

- Meet with the teacher or childcare provider at least twice a year (if there aren't regular conferences scheduled) to discuss the child's development. If it's not possible for you to attend a meeting, find another way to communicate.
- If you're fluent in more than one language, offer to translate flyers, policy handbooks, or other materials for parents who don't speak English. Give language lessons to children and teach them simple conversational phrases.

INFANTS

- Talk to childcare providers every day. Let them know how the infant is eating, sleeping during the night, napping, and so on. Ask for daily reports from caregivers, too.
- Volunteer to help feed babies at lunchtime.
- As requested by the childcare center, provide diapers, bottles, a change of clothing, or other items for the child. Include a blanket from home.
- If you are concerned about an infant's health or mood, call or visit when the infant is at childcare.
- Make a regular appointment to volunteer at a childcare center. Hold babies, read stories to toddlers, or play with older children. All children, including infants, thrive on personal attention from adults.

TODDLERS

- Let caregivers know if a child's routine changes—for example, if a parent is traveling on business or if a pet gets sick.
- Have flexible drop-off and pick-up times to help toddlers move smoothly from childcare to home and vice versa. Give children time to shift gears. Toddlers don't cope well with a "dump-and-run" approach.
- Ask local businesses or foundations to donate money or materials to the childcare setting. For example, a business doing remodeling could contribute used shelves.

- Suggest that the childcare center create a staff/parent advisory board (if there isn't one already) to meet regularly to discuss successes, needs, and challenges.
- Volunteer to spend time having fun with toddlers. Play with clay or dough. Read stories aloud. Build castles in the block area or roads in the sandbox.

PRESCHOOLERS

- Read all newspapers, notes, and printed announcements posted at the childcare center (or preschool) and those sent home with the child. Respond quickly to requests.
- Some preschools or childcare centers are nonprofit organizations. If so, donate funds if you can. Your contribution will be tax deductible.
- Call or contact the director of a preschool or childcare center to learn how you can show your support. If you are unable to contribute financially, you can help in other ways (by donating your time, for example).
- Offer to set up inexpensive field trips for the children. Help contact places in the community, such as the fire station, a bakery, the community library, a recycling center, or a horse ranch. Children can learn more about transportation by visiting an airport, a bus or train depot, a subway station, or a farm-equipment dealer. Volunteer to chaperone.
- Compliment or thank caregivers when they do something special (such as draw a picture for a preschooler) or when they get a haircut or share personal news. This shows you care about them as people.

ELEMENTARY-AGE CHILDREN

- Join the school's parent group and attend the meetings. Think of ways your skills can help the group. If you're good with a computer, for example, offer to set up a student directory including parent names and phone numbers. If you enjoy meeting new people, you might make phone calls to announce school events or recruit volunteers.

- Ask children about their homework each day and check to make sure they complete it. Set aside time to help when they need it.
- Attend open houses, inventors' fairs, and other school events. Make it a point to have casual conversations with teachers and other staff members.
- Ask your employer to support children and education. Advocate for flexible schedules so employees can volunteer at a school one hour per month, if they wish.
- If you're able, donate supplies for a classroom. (Ask the teacher for a list of suggestions.) Many classrooms need cups and plates for parties. Some like to use empty toilet paper tubes, margarine tubs, old magazines, and egg cartons for projects.

RESOURCE

National PTA
330 North Wabash Avenue, Suite 2100
Chicago, IL 60611
Toll-free phone: 1-800-307-4782
Web site: *www.pta.org/*

The mission of the National PTA is to support and speak on behalf of children and youth in the schools, help parents develop the skills they need to raise and protect their children, and encourage public involvement in public schools. Visit their Web site for information on a variety of topics, including safeguarding children in schools.

MORE IDEAS FOR BUILDING THE SUPPORT ASSETS

IDEAS FOR PARENTS

- Attend a parenting class or a workshop to learn new ways to support your children. Connect with other parents and talk about the challenges and rewards of parenting.
- Help extended family members get to know your child. Send letters about the child's activities, along with photos. Take your child along when you visit.
- Offer to become honorary aunts, uncles, or grandparents for children in your neighborhood, congregation, or social network.
- Have a regularly scheduled fun time. Record these important dates on a family calendar. Find something fun to do together—explore a park you've never visited, rent a paddle boat, or go snowshoeing.
- Refuel your personal support "tank" frequently. Spend time with a friend who makes you laugh. Take a long bath. Go for a walk by yourself. Shoot some hoops. Steal a few minutes to enjoy a magazine article.
- Be a partner in your child's education. Get to know your child's teacher or childcare provider. Work together to bring out the best in your child.
- Show attention and support through touch. Younger children enjoy hugs and snuggling, but older children like physical affection, too. Older children may prefer a back rub, an arm around their shoulders, or a pat on the back.
- Surround your children with caring adults. Always be on the lookout for adults who could take an interest in your child, and help build those relationships. Look for ways to support other people's children, too.

IDEAS FOR CHILDCARE PROVIDERS

- Each child should have a primary caregiver—an adult who cares for the child most of the time. This adult can give reports to the child's parents and make sure that the child's needs are being met.

- Light up and give children a big hello when you see them for the first time each day. Tell them how happy you are to see them.

- Learn the names of family members of children in your care. Go out of your way to welcome families during drop-off and pick-up times, even if you have children in your arms or need to say hello from across the room.

- Share simple ways that parents can support you as you care for their children. For example, if parents ask about your day in addition to the child's day, point out how much you appreciate that they care enough to ask.

- Spend a lot of time on the floor or close to the floor. Children will crawl into your lap when it's empty.

- When families have a new baby, send them a card or give them a call to congratulate them.

IDEAS FOR EDUCATORS

- Ask children to share information about themselves. For example, instead of show-and-tell, ask each child to talk about a specific personal topic, like "people in my family," "my pets," "my favorite book," and so on.

- Parents can be your teaching partners. Reach out to each child's parents and find out more about them. Learning about parents will tell you a lot about how you can support each child.

- Notice the type of support each child prefers. Some children like verbal affirmations. Others love a personal note.

- Create ways to include parents in your classroom. For example, a parent who travels a lot could send postcards to the class. A parent who works near the school may be able to read a story to the children during a lunch break.

- Ask children to list ways to show they care about other people. Their ideas might include taking turns, smiling, asking questions, and listening. Praise children when they do these things in your classroom.

ASSETS IN ACTION
School Coupons

Parents of elementary-school children in the Manchester School District (in Manchester, New Hampshire) received asset-building coupon books. These books were intended to raise parents' awareness of assets and to give practical suggestions for ways parents could build assets in their children. Each coupon had an asset-building activity that a child could "redeem" from her or his parents. For example, one coupon offered two hours of help with homework. Another coupon awarded children a supervised asset-building party at home.

IDEAS FOR HEALTH-CARE PROFESSIONALS

- Make sure health-care facilities are supportive and caring for all children, from newborns to teenagers. For example, have staff members greet children as well as caregivers.
- Support the decisions parents make and share ways they can provide what children need to grow up healthy and safe.
- Support community asset-building initiatives in any way you can. For example, cosponsor a children's asset fair or let organizers make informational flyers on your photocopy machine.
- Build relationships with patients who have chronic illnesses or need frequent care. Learn their names and something about them so you can chat with them anytime.

IDEAS FOR CONGREGATIONAL LEADERS

- Sit in a different place during each religious service so you can meet more families in the congregation. Talk to children nearby. If you must sit in a specific spot, consider inviting a different child to sit with you each time.

- Learn the names of children in your congregation. Say hello to them when you see them at services or in the community.
- Connect parents who have things in common. Start groups for parents who work outside the home, stay-at-home parents, parents of teenagers, parents of toddlers, and so on.
- Help children's teachers and caregivers build relationships with children and their families. Schedule regular "family nights" where families, caregivers, and teachers get together for fun activities.
- Teach lay leaders ways to support children. For example, have greeters welcome children as well as adults.

IDEAS FOR EMPLOYERS

- Help employees find ways to spend more time with their children. For example, a local dry cleaner or film processor could make regular pick-ups at your business, saving time for parents before or after work.
- Explore ways to support families needing childcare. Investigate the childcare options in your area and share the details with your employees.
- Think about the benefits you offer employees with children. How many people use them? If the benefits aren't popular, find out why. Make sure the benefits are truly helpful and that employees aren't being penalized for using them.
- Create ways for employees to participate in school activities during work hours. For example, some companies allow flexible scheduling or give employees paid time off to volunteer in a school or attend their children's school functions.
- Connect your business (and your employees) with a school, preschool, or childcare center. Consider supporting an athletic team or a children's music performance.

IDEAS FOR LIBRARIANS

- Create a comfortable family reading spot. Soft pillows, stuffed animals, and carpet squares make a cozy place for family members to enjoy books together.
- Sponsor a family library week with storytimes and other activities. Serve gingerbread cookies of different sizes to represent children and adults.
- Support families of prison inmates. Give prisoners access to audiotapes, recorders, and children's books so they can record stories for their children. Give the tapes and copies of the books to the children.
- Set up a reading buddy program to connect adults and teenagers with children. Have reading buddies meet once a month at the library to read stories together. Match up people who attend these events.
- Offer to read stories to children during school events so parents don't need to arrange childcare.

IDEAS FOR COMMUNITY LEADERS

- Have an annual baby shower where everyone gathers to meet the community's new babies. Let people mingle and celebrate the newest members of the community.
- Offer asset-building workshops to parents at convenient times and places. Schedule lunchtime sessions at a large company or morning meetings at a neighborhood center near many stay-at-home parents.
- Meet with agencies and service providers to learn more about how they help adults and children build relationships. Sponsor a service fair so community members can ask questions and get information about the programs.
- Help schools and agencies connect schoolchildren and older residents. Recruit a senior citizen to adopt a classroom, or—if more seniors are interested—pair each student with an elder buddy (a senior citizen mentor).

- Schedule an annual neighborhood get-together day. Each neighborhood or block club can have a party or a gathering where residents can meet and build relationships.

We encourage you to photocopy this page (set the image size at 125 percent), cut out the "Ideas for Children," and share them with a child you know.

IDEAS FOR CHILDREN: BUILD YOUR OWN SUPPORT ASSETS

- Smile and wave at people you know.
- Call someone you like and have a chat. If you don't like using the telephone, send a picture or postcard.
- Play games or start a club with your brothers and sisters and the children in your neighborhood.
- Talk to people you know in your neighborhood. Ask them questions like "How are you?" or "What are you doing?"
- Think about the things people do for you. Thank parents. Thank teachers. Thank coaches. Thank the people who take care of you.
- Talk about the things you like with your family and friends. Find out each other's favorite color, food, toy, game, music, movie, and book.
- Make something for a friend. Draw a picture. Create something with clay or Legos.

THE EMPOWERMENT
ASSETS

To feel that they're important and they belong, young children need safe and caring communities, schools, neighborhoods, and families surrounding them. When we help children act on their ideas and find ways to help others, we encourage them to grow and learn. When we listen to their thoughts and opinions, we show how much we value them.

The empowerment category includes four developmental assets for children from birth through age 11:

The Empowerment Assets

Asset 7: Community Values Children

Asset 8: Children Are Given Useful Roles

Asset 9: Service to Others

Asset 10: Safety

When Search Institute surveyed 6th graders, they found that children experience some of the empowerment assets more than others. Here are the percentages of these children who reported each of the assets in their lives:*

Asset 7: Community Values Youth   **33%**

Asset 8: Youth as Resources   **36%**

Asset 9: Service to Others   **61%**

Asset 10: Safety   **45%**

*Some of the asset names in the survey of 6th graders are different from those relating to younger children. The survey's asset names are the names that apply to older children and teens. The asset names in *What Young Children Need to Succeed* take into account developmental and situational differences of young children. See pages 3–5 for further information about asset language.

Asset 7

COMMUNITY VALUES CHILDREN

Parents and other adults in the community value and appreciate children.

How Search Institute defines this asset . . .

For infants: The family places infants at the center of family life. Other adults in the community value and appreciate infants.

For toddlers: The family places toddlers at the center of family life and recognizes the need to set limits for toddlers. Other adults in the community value and appreciate toddlers.

For preschoolers: Parents and other adults in the community value and appreciate preschoolers.

For elementary-age children: Children feel that the family and community value and appreciate children.

ALL CHILDREN

- Children spend many years learning to understand and express their emotions. Help them find appropriate ways to share their feelings with others.
- Do you know the old saying "Children should be seen and not heard"? Replace this with the idea that children should be seen, heard, and taken seriously.

- Spend time with children. Read books, play games, or take walks together. Let them know they're important.
- Keep track of the names of children on the holiday cards you receive. The next year, address the envelope to everyone in the family.

 DID YOU KNOW?

"Comprehensive community supports and services are necessary to ensure the healthy development of our youngest children." This statement comes from a report by the Carnegie Corporation of New York called *Starting Points: Meeting the Needs of Our Youngest Children*. To create a community that values children, the report suggests:

- creating neighborhood family and child centers that provide service and support for *all* families
- providing parent education and parenting support
- offering access to information and community services, such as quality childcare and comprehensive health services
- helping educate professionals who work with families
- strengthening collaboration among family programs, the business community, the media, and advocacy groups.

Source: *Starting Points: Meeting the Needs of Our Youngest Children* (New York: Carnegie Corporation of New York, 1994).

INFANTS

- When an infant cries, respond immediately. This teaches the infant that someone will take care of her.
- Crying, babbling, and cooing are all ways an infant communicates. Listen to the infant's sounds, and respond. If the baby babbles happily during a bath, for example, say, "You really like taking a bath, don't you?"

- An infant will let you know when he's hungry or needs a nap. Follow his schedule as much as possible.
- What are the infant's favorite comfort items? Does the baby have a special blanket or a stuffed toy? Make sure these favorites are always nearby. Bring them along on errands, visits, and trips.
- Hold the infant. Rock. Get down on the floor and shake a rattle. Take a break from everything else and just be together.

TODDLERS

- Be empathetic to toddlers' strong feelings about things. Listen to what they have to say and show them appropriate ways to express their emotions. Be calm when responding to toddlers—even when they aren't.
- When toddlers want to play, play. Honor their invitations and requests as much as you can.
- Let toddlers be toddlers. They like dumping out full containers. They like getting undressed. Find safe ways for toddlers to do the things they think are fun.
- Even the most energetic toddler gets tired and hungry. Be alert to cues that tell you this. For example, when a toddler rubs his eyes and cries, it might be time for a nap. Soothe him to sleep with a story or a song. If he's cranky or whiny, offer him a snack.

PRESCHOOLERS

- Let preschoolers "play pretend." Go along with the 3-year-old who suddenly turns into a superhero or the 4-year-old who becomes an executive.
- Enjoy what preschoolers draw and write. Encourage them to be creative. Delight in their creations without correcting them. You might say, "Look at all the beautiful colors you used in this drawing!" or "Can you tell me a story about the house you drew? I'll help you write it down."
- Preschoolers are proud of what they can do. Admire their skills when they say "Watch me!"

- Give preschoolers plenty of time to play, relax, and be alone.

- When a preschooler says monsters are under her bed, find out what's scaring her. Talk calmly with her about her feelings and help her handle her fears. It might help to create a sign that says "No Monsters Allowed!" and put it near her bed. Before bed each night, look under the bed together to check for monsters. Spend a few minutes talking or reading a story together before turning off the light.

RESOURCE

Connect for Kids
Web site: *www.connectforkids.org/*

Connect for Kids is a resource for adults who want to make their communities better places for kids. Visit this comprehensive Web site for information on volunteer programs, learning development, what's new in your state, and other ideas and tools to help improve children's lives.

ELEMENTARY-AGE CHILDREN

- Give children some control over a part of their day. Set aside time for them to play soccer, braid yarn, or do another activity *they* choose to do.

- Ask for children's opinions and suggestions. Use some of their ideas.

- When you see families you know, talk to each person—including the children. Get everyone involved in the conversation.

- Tell children when you see them doing something you appreciate or value. You might say, "It's really great that you care enough to pick up litter."

ASSETS IN ACTION
Valuing Children from Infancy

The community library in St. Louis Park, Minnesota, has a program called "Happy Birthday One-Year-Olds!" On the second Monday of each month, parents bring their birthday babies to a 20-minute morning program. The parents and children hear a story, learn how to get a library card, and look at books written for infants. Each infant then receives a book as a gift, provided by the Friends of the Library.

Asset 8

CHILDREN ARE GIVEN USEFUL ROLES

Parents involve children in family life in ways that fit children's needs and abilities. Preschool and elementary-age children have useful roles at home and in the community and have a voice in family decisions.

How Search Institute defines this asset . . .

For infants and toddlers: The family involves infants and toddlers in family life.

For preschoolers: Parents and other adults create ways preschoolers can help out and gradually include preschoolers in age-appropriate tasks.

For elementary-age children: Children are included in age-appropriate family tasks and decisions and are given useful roles at home and in the community.

ALL CHILDREN

- Show your love and concern for children.
- Give children plenty of safe space to explore and play.
- Let children know that every person can contribute to the family. Assign children age-appropriate chores or have them help with small projects. Completing simple tasks gives a child a sense of accomplishment. For example, a 3-year-old can bring napkins to the table. An 8-year-old can wash lettuce for a salad while a 10-year-old makes sandwiches.

INFANTS

- Arrange family life around the infant's needs. Adults should adapt to a newborn's schedule before gradually getting the child to settle into a regular routine.
- Smile at an infant. Have your face about 8 to 12 inches from him. Show how happy you are when the infant smiles back at you.
- When you're around to watch, lay a young infant on her stomach to give her practice holding up her head. Stop the activity when she starts to fuss or gets sleepy. (Never leave an unsupervised infant on her stomach.)
- Speak to babies as you play with them, change their diapers, bathe them, and feed them. Talk about what you're doing together.

RESOURCE

On the Day You Were Born by Debra Frasier (New York: Harcourt Brace, 1997) shows a child his important place in the family and in the world. Read this gentle picture book aloud to welcome infants and toddlers to the world; older children can read it for themselves.

TODDLERS

- Let toddlers play with cupboard doors and other things that have hinges. Swinging things strengthens a toddler's coordination.
- Give toddlers simple tasks to do, such as bringing Dad his shoes from the doormat or putting blocks into a bucket.
- Record a toddler singing a lullaby or a favorite song and play the tape for infants.

PRESCHOOLERS

- Find ways for preschoolers to show they're part of a family. For example, buy plain white T-shirts and nontoxic fabric markers and help preschoolers make matching shirts for themselves and family members.

- Let preschoolers create posters, pictures, and cards for someone's birthday or a holiday.

- Have older preschoolers draw a picture of a type of toy (such as a car) to tape to a bucket or another storage container. Have them create labels for each kind of toy so they know where their toys belong and can put them away easily. (Younger preschoolers can help an adult place a drawing or a photo of the toy on the container.)

- Be patient when preschoolers don't finish tasks. They often forget and just need reminding. Other times they may resist because they're upset about something else. Instead of getting annoyed, find out what the problem is and help the preschooler solve it.

- Ask for a preschooler's help in planning a family event, like a birthday party or reunion.

ELEMENTARY-AGE CHILDREN

- Find ways to put children in charge. For example, children can plan and lead games at a birthday party or a neighborhood block party. (Make sure plenty of willing children and adults are around to help out.)

- Have children help you with projects, such as painting a bathroom, cleaning out a drawer, or planting bulbs in a flower bed.

- Ask children to teach you new things. Can they show you a new swimming stroke or a magic trick?

- If you have access to the Internet, check out Web sites developed by children for children. You can find a helpful list at *home.about.com/kidsteens/*, or access a search engine for more ideas. (Talk with children and set rules about using the Internet safely beforehand. If you're concerned that children may view inappropriate material, purchase a filtering program or visit a site like the New York Institute for Special Education's safety page at *www.nyise.org/safety* for more information.)

- Children will be ready for more challenges as they grow older. For example, a kindergartner can put away clean socks in a drawer, while an 11-year-old can strip the bed and make sure all his dirty clothes are in the hamper.
- Let a child make choices, such as occasionally deciding what the family will have for dinner or setting the time for a visit to the public library.

ASSETS IN ACTION
Giving Children a Voice

When Mary Goulette worked with a corporation to raise money for 10 elementary schools in her area, she took the fund-raiser a step further to empower the children at the schools. Mary had students at each school vote on how they wanted the money to be spent. For example, one school held a diversity night for families and served a spaghetti dinner. At another, the kids voted to expand the outdoor playground. A 5-year-old student proudly held a large replica of the check at the dedication ceremony for the new equipment.

Asset 9

SERVICE TO OTHERS

Together, parents and children serve others in the community.

How Search Institute defines this asset . . .

For infants and toddlers: Parents serve others in the community.

For preschoolers: The family serves others in the community together.

For elementary-age children: Children serve others in the community with their family or in other settings.

ALL CHILDREN

- Get involved in service projects. When children see adults helping others, they're more likely to do it themselves.
- Do your best to meet children's needs. Besides being fed and clothed, children need to feel valued and cared for. Then, when they're older, they'll be more willing to meet the needs of others.
- Create ways for children and their parents to serve together. For example, families can transport donated toys, send holiday cards, or rake leaves.
- Thank children who serve others. Tell them what you appreciate about their contribution.

INFANTS

- Focus on a baby and meet all of her needs. This lays the foundation for the infant to grow into a child who wants to give to others.
- If you're in charge of service opportunities, keep them short and simple for parents of infants. No matter what the service is, the infants' needs should always come first.
- When it's appropriate, bring infants along when volunteering at a nursing home or sorting donations at a food shelf.
- Suggest simple service projects that parents can do at home. For example, they might sew pillowcases for a shelter or saw wooden pieces into shapes for children's toys.
- Ask parents to donate infant clothes, baby shampoo, or jars of baby food to organizations, if they're able.

TODDLERS

- Families with toddlers can serve in easy ways. They're more likely to enjoy spending time together if they're not expected to get a lot done quickly.
- Arrange for other adults to care for and play with toddlers while their parents do service projects.
- Find simple ways for toddlers to serve others. For example, they may be able to place donated toys in a box.
- Talk about and demonstrate what it means to share and take turns. Be patient and understand that children won't grasp this concept right away.

PRESCHOOLERS

- Ask preschoolers to draw pictures on folded paper to make greeting cards. Send these cards along with donated items.
- Take preschoolers along when visiting sick and elderly people. Have preschoolers bring their favorite toys to talk about and share.
- Record preschoolers singing songs and telling stories. Send a copy of the recording to cheer up a sick relative.

- Ask preschoolers to draw pictures of the things they do to help others. Say, "Can you tell me what's happening in your drawing?"
- Invite preschoolers to collect mittens, toys, or bandages for organizations that can use them. Have groups of adults and preschoolers collect contributions door-to-door. Let preschoolers take turns pulling the wagon holding the donations.

 DID YOU KNOW?

Getting children started volunteering at an early age is a way to nurture an ongoing interest in service. Researchers at the Independent Sector say, "Volunteering is an activity most likely to be cultivated in childhood and during the early teenage years." Of teenagers who volunteer, 34 percent first started before the age of 12. Another 25 percent started volunteering between the ages of 12 and 13.

Source: *Volunteering and Giving Among Teenagers 12 to 17 Years of Age* (Washington, DC: Independent Sector, 1997).

ELEMENTARY-AGE CHILDREN

- Ask children to list some ways they can serve others. Then help them act on their ideas.
- Create service projects that let children spend time with other people. For example, they might play with children in a congregational nursery or read a story to a resident at a health-care center.
- Have older children distribute programs at a school event or play. (Younger children can team up with adults to do this.)
- A child and his family could help a relative or neighbor by running an errand, raking leaves, doing laundry, cooking a meal, shoveling a sidewalk, or taking out the trash.

- Encourage children to keep a journal of stories and pictures about their volunteer experiences. Even younger elementary-age children can usually write a few sentences or draw a picture about what they've done. Together, look through the journal and let the child tell you about what she's written.

RESOURCES

Children as Volunteers by Susan J. Ellis, Anne Weisbord, and Katherine H. Noyes (Philadelphia: Energize, 1991) gives creative ways for children of different ages to do service projects with their families and in schools or clubs.

The Kid's Guide to Service Projects by Barbara A. Lewis (Minneapolis: Free Spirit Publishing, 1995) includes over 500 service projects for young people who want to make a difference. For ages 10 and up (younger children can do many of these projects with the help of an adult).

ASSETS IN ACTION
Empowering Children—and Adults

At a manufacturing plant in Newark, Ohio, workers can take an hour of paid time each week to mentor a child at a local elementary school. "We give employees the time and provide backup so they can leave the job," says Al Ernest, department manager. As workers begin spending time with kids, he notes, they realize they have a lot to give. "The mentoring program shows that they have a responsibility and that they can add value to the community," Al says. "It lets them know that they have a lot to offer."

Asset 10

SAFETY

Homes, schools, childcare settings, and other environments are safe for children.

How Search Institute defines this asset . . .

For infants, toddlers, and preschoolers: Children have safe environments at home, in out-of-home settings, and in the neighborhood. This includes childproofing* these environments.

For elementary-age children: Children are safe at home, at school, and in the neighborhood.

ALL CHILDREN

- Create an atmosphere where children feel cared for and emotionally safe. Play with them and let them know you care.
- When a child is afraid, comfort him. A hug or a cuddle can help him feel secure and protected.
- Keep a close eye on children's play, especially at playgrounds and near stairs and windows.

---

* For information on childproofing, see page 78.

- Be a role model—and keep yourself safe—by always using your seat belt in the car.

- Supervise children carefully when they're around water—even a large puddle can be dangerous for a small child. If you're on a boat, make sure everyone wears a life jacket that fits properly. Register older children for swimming lessons.

RESOURCES

The National SAFE KIDS Campaign
1301 Pennsylvania Avenue NW, Suite 1000
Washington, DC 20004-1707
Telephone: (202) 662-0600
Web site: *www.safekids.org*

The National SAFE KIDS Campaign claims that as many as 90 percent of unintentional childhood injuries can be prevented. The Campaign's goal is to teach adults how to make their community safer for children of all ages. Contact the organization for fact sheets, safety tips, and other educational materials and to learn how you can join or start a SAFE KIDS coalition in your area.

KidsHealth.org
Web site: *www.kidshealth.org*

This is one of the largest sites on the Internet that provides expert health information about children from before birth through adolescence. Created by The Nemours Foundation Center for Children's Health Media, this reliable, up-to-date, and entertaining site includes hundreds of in-depth articles and features about ways to keep kids healthy and safe.

INFANTS

- Accidents can happen easily and quickly, so keep a close eye on infants. An infant who is learning to crawl, stand, or walk may bump into something or take a tumble. Even newborns can be hurt if left unattended.

- When laying an infant down to sleep, place her on her back or side. The American Academy of Pediatrics reports that infants who sleep on their stomachs are at higher risk for Sudden Infant Death Syndrome (SIDS).
- Protect infants from siblings who may not know how to be gentle around a baby. Keep babies away from pets who might bite, swat, or scratch.
- Move dangerous items (such as a cup of hot coffee) far from an infant's grasping hands.
- Childproof the infant's home and other places where he spends time. (Ask a pediatrician or a childcare provider for tips on how to do this.)
- Keep an infant safely seated in the car. The National Highway and Transportation Safety Board specifies that infants up to 20 pounds and up to 1 year old ride in the back seat in a rear-facing child seat.

TODDLERS

- Keep track of toddlers at all times. They can dash into streets, leap from furniture, or knock over glass dishes in the blink of an eye.
- Keep toddlers away from small toys and objects so they don't swallow them or choke. Teach children to bring small items to an adult instead of putting the objects in their mouths.
- Develop new and creative childproofing strategies as toddlers figure out how to open doors with childproof latches and how to remove outlet covers. For example, some special childproof latches can only be opened by a magnetic key. If you need more ideas, a pediatrician or childcare provider might have some suggestions.
- Toddlers' bodies may not be coordinated enough to do some tasks. Expect toddlers to fall now and then, but watch them closely so they don't seriously hurt themselves.
- When a toddler bites or hits, step in right away and let the child know that this behavior is inappropriate. Be firm, but don't embarrass or shame her. Help her learn how to find words for her feelings.

DID YOU KNOW?

Here are a few simple things you can do to start childproofing your home:

- Store medicines, household cleaners, poisons, and plastic bags in a locked childproof cabinet or container.
- Never leave water in a sink or tub. Install safety latches on toilets so children can't open them.
- Seal all unused electrical outlets with childproof covers. Move electrical cords out of the reach of children.
- Use safety covers on stove and oven knobs, and keep handles of pots on the stove turned inward, away from small hands.
- Post a list of emergency numbers (including the local poison control center and the nearest hospital) near every phone in the home.
- Install safety gates near all stairways.

PRESCHOOLERS

- Talk with preschoolers about fear. Find out what their fears are. Help them become comfortable with their feelings. Say, "It's okay to be scared. Everyone is afraid sometimes."
- Teach a preschooler his first and last name, address, and phone number. To help him learn more quickly, set the information to a familiar tune.
- Explain that some body parts are private. Tell children that only parents, caregivers, and health-care workers should be allowed to see these parts (with the preschooler's permission). Encourage children to tell a trusted adult immediately if anyone ever touches them in ways that make them feel uncomfortable.

- Praise preschoolers when they buckle the belts on car-safety seats without being asked. Emphasize how grown-up they're acting. (The National Highway and Transportation Safety Board recommends that children ride in safety seats until they're 4'9" or 80 pounds.)
- Teach preschoolers the phone number 911 (*nine-one-one*, not *nine-eleven*). Talk about what an emergency is—and isn't.

ELEMENTARY-AGE CHILDREN

- Talk to children about strangers. Ask, "What can you do if someone makes you feel afraid or worried?" Help children develop their own personal plans to handle unsafe situations. Teach children who they can go to when they feel scared or need help: teachers, cashiers, police officers, fire fighters, security guards, and so on.
- Help children feel comfortable when they're away from home—at school, at after-school activities, and at friends' homes. If they feel unsafe, what can they do to ease their fears? Brainstorm some ideas.
- Children should always wear helmets while riding a bike or skating. Make sure children have the appropriate protective gear for the sports they play—and that they use and wear it correctly.
- Tell children how much you appreciate it when they buckle their safety belts without being reminded.
- Teach a child the correct spelling of her first and last name. Help her learn how to spell her address and write her phone number.
- Use the buddy system. Have children play or go places in pairs.

ASSETS IN ACTION
Empowering New Parents

When parents leave a hospital with a newborn, they also take home information about poisons, warning signs of serious illnesses, immunizations and their side effects, and other problems.

Parents who give birth at Holy Family Hospital in New Richmond, Wisconsin, get something more: a colorful set of 10 building blocks. Eight of the blocks feature the eight asset categories. Another block says, "Smile and be resilient." The final block says, "Building developmental assets begins at birth and lasts a lifetime."

In addition, parents receive a manila envelope labeled "Notice: Valuable Information to Use with Your Blocks." The envelope includes an asset-building bookmark called "Building Blocks for Life," the list of 40 developmental assets for infants and toddlers, a copy of a brochure about asset building, and a booklet on becoming an asset-building parent.*

The hospital also takes a picture of the last baby born each year to use for publicity. "As a community, we often make a big deal about the first baby born each year," says Marilyn Peplau, an asset-building initiative team member. "But asset building is about all children—from the firstborn to the last."

---

* A brochure called *The Asset Approach* and a booklet for parents called *Parenting with a Purpose* are available from Search Institute. For more information, see pages 298 and 303–304.

MORE IDEAS FOR BUILDING THE EMPOWERMENT ASSETS

IDEAS FOR PARENTS

- Have an older child draw a picture of your family. Hang it in a place of honor in your home or near a younger child's crib or bed.
- Take "talking turns" while you watch a television program or movie at home together. Give each member of the family a chance to say something about the program. Listen to everyone's comments without criticizing.
- Give children a large box to fill with toys they no longer use. Let children choose what to keep and what to give away. Donate the box of toys (those in good condition) to a charity.
- Develop a dinner-bell chain. When dinner is ready, the cook tells one family member. That person tells another person, and so on.
- Display or use things your child makes. A clay bowl can hold loose change. A decorated cup can hold flowers.

IDEAS FOR CHILDCARE PROVIDERS

- Look at the environment from a child's perspective. Hang coat racks or pegs low enough so children can reach their own coats. Some childcare centers have even installed child-sized toilets for toddlers to use.
- Set aside some time each day when children can choose what they want to do.
- Take photographs of children at your childcare center. Display the photos for children and parents to enjoy.
- Childproof every room. Have safety gates in doorways. Supervise children closely, particularly those who can remove safety latches.

- Teach children about strangers by showing them pictures of people they know and people they don't know. (Include pictures of smiling strangers—some young children don't think happy-looking strangers are actually strangers.) Explain that children can talk to strangers only when they're with an adult they know.

IDEAS FOR EDUCATORS

- Have a weekly talk time where children take turns saying something personal about themselves. Topics might be their favorite game, a hero they admire, or something they're proud of.
- On each child's birthday, draw a cake on a large piece of construction paper. Have children sit on the floor while the birthday child sits in a special "birthday chair." Ask other children to say what they like about the child. Write the comments on the paper along with the names of who said what. Give the paper to the birthday child.
- Create a scrapbook or photo album of classroom service projects.
- Videotape a class play or a special class project. Find a volunteer to make copies for families who provide a videotape. Ask families to donate tapes for parents who can't afford them.
- Whenever you send home permission forms for parents to sign, consider adding a line where children can sign, too.

IDEAS FOR HEALTH-CARE PROFESSIONALS

- Have a sticker basket or a toy drawer handy. Children can choose an item as a treat after an appointment.
- Talk to patients, especially children, about an examination or procedure before you start. After explaining what they can expect, ask for permission to begin. Ask patients how they're feeling if they seem uncomfortable. For example, older children may still be nervous about immunizations. Calm their fears and answer their questions.
- Ask older children to help you design child-friendly examination and waiting areas. Children often have good ideas that may not occur to adults.

- Childproof all waiting areas, examination rooms, and hall-ways to make them safe for infants, toddlers, preschoolers, and elementary-age children.
- Others respect you and are likely to follow your example, so share your asset-building ideas. Initiatives you develop can reach many members of the community.

IDEAS FOR CONGREGATIONAL LEADERS

- Ask children to be leaders at services. They might be greeters or ushers, hand out programs, or do readings.
- Have children brainstorm and choose ideas for service projects.
- Childproof the worship area, the social hall, and other places where families gather.
- Ask children to give money to the congregation or to charities on a regular basis, if they're able.
- Let children in your congregation design the bulletin cover or pictures within the bulletin on special occasions.
- Observe special days your faith community sets aside for children. For example, some congregations celebrate the Children's Sabbath on the third Sunday of October. To learn more, contact the Children's Defense Fund, 25 E Street NW, Washington, DC 20001; telephone: (202) 662-3652; Web site: *www.childrensdefense.org*.

IDEAS FOR EMPLOYERS

- Encourage employees to bring their children to the workplace sometimes. (A popular time for this is Take Our Daughters to Work Day, which is celebrated on the fourth Thursday in April. Many parents bring their daughters *and* sons to work with them on this day.) Plan activities for children to take part in when they visit.
- Set out a bowl of small, safe toys for young visitors. Talk with children who come through the door and offer them a toy.
- If an employee's child is mentioned in the newspaper, send the child and the parents a note of congratulation.

- Employees do more than just work. Recognize their roles as mentors, volunteers, aunts, uncles, parents, and community members.
- Support educational and community efforts that help children. Give your time, money, and expertise.
- Encourage employees to display their children's artwork in their work areas.
- Throw a company baby shower for employees who become new parents. Decorate their work space.

IDEAS FOR LIBRARIANS

- Make sure that the children's section of your library is child-friendly and fun. Set out buckets of board books for toddlers. Have stuffed animals and puppets (keep them clean and in good repair) for children to cuddle with. Are books and other materials placed where children can see and reach them easily? Are chairs, tables, and reading areas designed for children?
- Have children create library book displays and bookmarks. Hold a contest and award prizes to everyone who enters.
- Encourage children to check out books from the library. Visit all the 1st-grade classes in area schools to talk about the library. Help children register for their own library cards.
- After a library book sale, donate leftover children's books to a childcare center or preschool.
- Keep bathrooms clean and safe. (Schedule more frequent bathroom cleanings if many children visit your library.) Provide a changing table and toddler potty chair in both the men's and women's rest rooms.

IDEAS FOR COMMUNITY LEADERS

- Schedule an annual community baby shower to celebrate all the babies born or adopted in the past year.
- Have toy items handy so young children can help with service projects. For example, give children miniature shovels to use while adults work on a community garden.

ASSETS IN ACTION
Children Helping Children

In Minnetonka, Minnesota, the We Can Ride Program teamed up juvenile offenders at a county correctional facility with disabled children. Both the teens and the children were empowered by the opportunities this relationship created. Troubled teens found a sense of pride and began to open up as they helped the children get on horses and ride them. At the same time, the children felt valued by the teenagers while they enjoyed their new successful roles as horseback riders.

- Keep parks and playgrounds clean, safe, and well lighted. Fix damaged playground equipment immediately.
- Use your community newspaper or a community bulletin board to recognize people who make a difference for children.
- Get children's input and feedback on community decisions, whether you're building a playground or planning a community parade.
- Have an annual community service project day. Encourage businesses, organizations, and congregations to choose different service projects and do them on the same day. Celebrate as a group afterward.

We encourage you to photocopy this page (set the image size at 125 percent), cut out the "Ideas for Children," and share them with a child you know.

IDEAS FOR CHILDREN:
BUILD YOUR OWN EMPOWERMENT ASSETS

- Talk about the things that are important to you. Let people know what you think.

- What can you do to help someone else? If you aren't sure, ask an adult for ideas.

- Keep yourself safe. Make sure that an adult always knows where you are. If you feel afraid, talk to an adult you trust.

- Listen to what other people have to say. Ask questions.

- Thank people who do helpful things.

- Tell your family about safety lessons you learn.

- Can you think of ways to make your neighborhood better? Share your ideas with an adult and make a plan together. You can make a difference!

THE BOUNDARIES AND EXPECTATIONS ASSETS

Knowing what's expected of them—and what's not—helps children create, learn, and grow. Instead of holding children back, limits keep them safe and secure. When they know who to count on and how to behave, children can concentrate on developing and learning new skills.

The boundaries and expectations category includes six developmental assets for children from birth through age 11:

The Boundaries and Expectations Assets

Asset 11: Family Boundaries

Asset 12: Out-of-Home Boundaries

Asset 13: Neighborhood Boundaries

Asset 14: Adult Role Models

Asset 15: Positive Peer Interaction and Influence

Asset 16: Appropriate Expectations for Growth

When Search Institute surveyed 6th graders, they found that children experience some of the boundaries and expectations assets more than others. Here are the percentages of these children who reported each of the assets in their lives:*

Asset 11: Family Boundaries	**49%**
Asset 12: School Boundaries	**70%**
Asset 13: Neighborhood Boundaries	**59%**
Asset 14: Adult Role Models	**35%**
Asset 15: Positive Peer Influence	**82%**
Asset 16: High Expectations	**59%**

*Some of the asset names in the survey of 6th graders are different from those relating to younger children. The survey's asset names are the names that apply to older children and teens. The asset names in *What Young Children Need to Succeed* take into account developmental and situational differences of young children. See pages 3–5 for further information about asset language.

Asset 11

FAMILY BOUNDARIES

Parents understand children's needs and preferences, model appropriate behavior, and set age-appropriate limits and consequences.

How Search Institute defines this asset . . .

For infants: Parents are aware of infants' preferences and adapt the environment and schedule to suit infants' needs. Parents begin setting limits as infants become mobile.

For toddlers: Parents are aware of toddlers' preferences and adapt the environment to suit toddlers' needs. Parents set age-appropriate limits for toddlers.

For preschoolers: The family has clear rules and consequences. The family monitors preschoolers and consistently demonstrates appropriate behavior through modeling and limit setting.

For elementary-age children: The family has clear rules and consequences and monitors children's activities and whereabouts.

ALL CHILDREN

- Use discipline to point children toward good behavior and appropriate decisions. Praise children when they do the right thing. Focus on the positive instead of the negative.
- Don't spank, hit, or shake a child. This teaches that it's okay to hit other people. Instead, model how you want the child to

behave. Be calm. Put your feelings into words. If you're frustrated, take a moment to relax before you speak.

- Always show a child how much you love him. Never withhold love as a form of discipline.

- A child will not fully understand boundaries until late adolescence. As children grow, their boundaries need to grow with them in developmentally appropriate ways. Revise boundaries as children learn to make age-appropriate decisions.

RESOURCES

Your Seven-Year-Old, Your Eight-Year-Old, Your Nine-Year-Old, and *Your Ten-to-Fourteen-Year Old* by Louise Bates Ames, Ph.D., and Frances L. Ilg, M.D. (New York: Dell, 1987, 1990, 1997, 1989), help parents and other adults understand normal development and behavior for children at certain ages. The series also includes books about younger children, from infancy to 6 years old.

INFANTS

- Recognize that infants are too young to understand boundaries and limits. An infant who cries isn't misbehaving, she's distressed about something—she might be wet, tired, or hungry.

- Childproof your home. Make it a safe place with clear boundaries for infants.

- Distracting a baby—giving the infant something different to focus on—is a good way to set boundaries or limits. For example, if an infant is grabbing your hair, wave a toy for him to pull on instead. Distraction usually works best before the age of 7½ months. For an older infant, remove toys or objects (if they're the cause of the problem) and guide the child to a more appropriate activity.

- Author Burton L. White, Ph.D., suggests beginning to set limits for infants between the ages of 7½ and 10 months. Set boundaries by changing the environment or the situation. For example, when an infant crawls toward an electrical cord, move furniture so the cord is hidden or move the baby to a different place that's childproofed.

RESOURCES

The First Twelve Months of Life (revised and updated), *The Second Twelve Months of Life,* and *The Early Childhood Years* by Frank Caplan and Theresa Caplan, The Princeton Center for Infancy and Early Childhood (New York: Bantam Books, 1995, 1979, 1984), are classics in child development, covering what infants know at each stage of development and what parents can do to help them grow and thrive.

The New First Three Years of Life by Burton L. White, Ph.D. (New York: Simon and Schuster, 1995), provides a summary of how a child develops and stresses the importance of loving but firm parenting.

Touchpoints by T. Berry Brazelton, M.D. (New York: Addison Wesley Longman, 1992), answers many questions parents have about their child's behavior, feelings, and development over the first few years.

TODDLERS

- Keep instructions and limits simple and positive.
- Calmly repeat simple rules when toddlers don't follow them. Expect toddlers to need many reminders.
- Some toddlers will be ready for toilet training earlier than others. Toilet training most likely won't be successful in early toddlerhood, and pushing children too early will only prolong the process, says the American Academy of Pediatrics. Let toddlers know what you expect of them, but be patient with the inevitable accidents.
- Calm toddlers when they can't control themselves. For example, say, "You're upset. You're running in circles and can't stop. Let's calm down." Then take the child by the hand and sit down to read or just snuggle for a few minutes.

DID YOU KNOW?

Research psychologists at the National Institute of Mental Health have found that the way a parent disciplines a child has a big influence on the child's developing conscience. Toddlers are more likely to comply with parents' requests when parents:

- give clear limits
- promote sympathy and compassion for others
- provide clear instructions and explanations about how to behave.

These methods are much more successful than threats or physical punishments.

Source: Leon Kuczynski and Grazyna Kochanska, "Development of Children's Non-Compliance Strategies from Toddlerhood to Age 5." *Developmental Psychology* 26 (1990).

PRESCHOOLERS

- Be imaginative and positive when enforcing boundaries. For example, you might say, "I see you're a lumberjack. Can you use your muscles to lift all those heavy toys and put them in the lumberjack's toy box?"
- Expect preschoolers to resist daily routines at times. Talk with them about their behavior and teach them the words they need to say how they feel. Ask children for better ways to do things.
- Be reasonable when setting boundaries. Too many boundaries can make a child feel stifled and powerless. Too few can make a child feel lost and out of control. Change boundaries that don't work.
- See which discipline methods the child responds to best. Some children do well with a time-out. Others need a stern talk. Make it clear that the child's behavior, not the child herself, is unacceptable.
- Learn to be *authoritative*—to set limits and offer choices without being too strict or too permissive.

- Preschoolers sometimes swear, lie, and exaggerate. Don't ignore these behaviors, but don't come down too hard on children. Preschoolers do these things to exercise their new-found feelings of independence. Point out that these behaviors are inappropriate. Correct children, then put the episode behind you.

RESOURCES

The Explosive Child by Ross W. Greene, Ph.D. (New York: HarperCollins, 1998), discusses the origins of children's "melt-downs" and presents strategies to help prevent them.

Guiding Young Children's Behavior, edited by Betty Farber, M.Ed. (Cutchogue, NY: Preschool Publications, 1997), gathers knowledge from 28 early childhood experts to help parents and teachers find realistic and gentle ways to respond to preschoolers' energy, creativity, and ingenuity.

How to Handle a Hard-to-Handle Kid by C. Drew Edwards, Ph.D. (Minneapolis: Free Spirit Publishing, 1999), teaches readers about different styles of parental discipline (authoritative, authoritarian, and permissive) identified by Diana Baumarind, Ph.D.

ELEMENTARY-AGE CHILDREN

- Help children develop a daily routine. Coordinating many schedules may be difficult, but do your best to make some parts of the day predictable.
- When children exaggerate and act in dramatic ways, acknowledge their feelings. Listen to what they're trying to say instead of correcting them.
- Pay attention to the messages you're sending. Children can sense when you're stressed or distracted. Children often act inappropriately when they're not getting enough attention or when they think you're concerned about something else.
- Talk with children about behaviors you both see on television or in public. Ask children what they think is appropriate and inappropriate and why.

- Teach children to listen to their bodies. Point out that they have trouble concentrating when they're tired or get crabby when they're hungry. Help children learn how to take care of themselves. For example, show them how to make a simple snack or meal, like a peanut butter and jelly sandwich.

- Anticipate an increase in inappropriate behavior during stressful family times and when family members are ill. Be understanding, and help the child find healthy ways to cope.

Asset 12

OUT-OF-HOME BOUNDARIES

Out-of-home environments provide age-appropriate activities and rest times and have clear rules and consequences.

How Search Institute defines this asset . . .

For infants: Childcare settings and other out-of-home environments have clear rules and consequences for older infants and consistently provide all infants with appropriate stimulation and enough rest.

For toddlers and preschoolers: Childcare settings and other out-of-home environments have clear rules and consequences to protect toddlers and preschoolers while consistently providing appropriate stimulation and enough rest.

For elementary-age children: Schools and other out-of-home environments provide clear rules and consequences.

ALL CHILDREN

- Talk to caregivers, teachers, and other adults about the purpose of boundaries and discipline. These things help direct children toward appropriate activities and away from inappropriate ones.

- Keep boundaries clear and enforce them consistently. When boundaries change, this confuses children and they don't know how to act.
- Stay positive—say yes more often than you say no. Give children positive feedback when they act in appropriate ways.
- Stay calm when setting and enforcing boundaries. Yelling triggers yelling.
- Be patient with yourself when setting and enforcing boundaries. Sometimes you'll lose your temper. When this happens, accept it, own up to it, apologize, and move on. Adults who show that people can lose their temper without going out of control also teach children an important lesson.

 DID YOU KNOW?

According to surveys by the American Psychological Association, some people believe that children need to be spanked sometimes. They see spanking as a way to make children behave, but research shows that it's better to reward positive behavior instead of punishing negative acts. Additionally, children who are spanked are more likely to use force to control other people when they're older. Instead of spanking children, adults should use time-outs or other non-violent forms of discipline.

Source: American Psychological Association Task Force on Violence and the Family (Washington, DC: American Psychological Association, 1994); Web site: *www.apa.org/*.

INFANTS

- Ask caregivers how they feel about boundaries for infants. Do they understand that infants don't break rules on purpose?
- Use distraction as the main method of setting boundaries for infants. If an infant's toy is inappropriate, give him something else to play with. If he keeps getting into an unsafe place, move him to a different area.

- Be calm and loving when setting a boundary for an infant.
- Get down on the floor regularly and check the environment from the infant's point of view. Are boundaries clear and safe?

TODDLERS

- Look at why a toddler may be acting inappropriately before you discipline her. Is she hungry? tired? overstimulated? frustrated with a toy?
- Be firm when an out-of-bounds toddler gives you an impish grin. Don't let "cute" behavior change boundaries—or how you enforce them.
- Realize that toddlers have limited memories. That's why it's important to repeat boundaries (often several times a day for many weeks).
- Give toddlers alternatives to inappropriate behavior. Share some ideas about how to act.

PRESCHOOLERS

- Create appropriate consequences for out-of-bounds behavior. For example, if a preschooler throws toys, have him pick up the toys and apologize to his playmates. Say, "It's important to play nicely with our friends. Please say you're sorry for throwing toys." If he doesn't want to do this, take away a privilege until he does.
- Notice when thumb-suckers and blanket-carriers seem ready to let go of these behaviors. Help them find other positive ways to comfort themselves or handle their feelings. Encourage them to share their feelings with adults.
- Help preschoolers use words instead of actions to express their wants, needs, and feelings. For example, say, "I don't know what you want when you jump up and down. If you'd like a cookie, please ask for one."
- Give preschoolers ideas about how to act appropriately. Try to keep calm when setting and enforcing boundaries, even with preschoolers who seem to have trouble doing what you ask.

Sometimes it helps to offer a child a choice. For example, "Do you want to pick up your toys *before* or *after* you get dressed?"

Elementary-Age Children

- Learn about school rules and boundaries. If you aren't sure what these are, ask a school administrator or a classroom teacher.

- A couple of months into the school year, ask children what they think of classroom boundaries. Are the boundaries too strict or lenient? Talk about ways to make adjustments. Share their ideas with a school teacher or administrator.

- Give children opportunities to role-play situations and discuss appropriate and inappropriate ways to respond. For example, if a child sees another child being bullied, what will the child do? An inappropriate response would be to join in. An appropriate response would be to get away from the situation as quickly as possible and get help from an adult.

RESOURCE

Positive Discipline in the Classroom by Jane Nelsen, Lynn Lott, and H. Stephen Glenn (Rocklin, CA: Prima, 1997) offers helpful ways to set and enforce boundaries at school while respecting students and setting appropriate expectations.

- Parents need to know when a child has been sent to the principal's office for misbehavior. Together, the child's parents and school staff members can teach the child better ways to act.

- Ask school districts and bus companies to set clear guidelines for children's behavior on the school bus. Let parents know these guidelines so families can discuss them before the school year starts. Make sure bus drivers know these guidelines and can enforce them effectively and consistently. If problems arise, bus drivers should have someone to turn to for support.

- When children are doing well at upholding boundaries, begin to train them as peer mediators so they can share their skills with others.

ASSETS IN ACTION
Meeting the Peacekeepers

Some children are scared of police officers, even though they know that these adults are there to protect them. Officer Rex McChesney of the Clear Lake, Iowa, police department helps teach children that police officers are their friends. He and other officers have been visiting kindergarten classes regularly for the past nine years. "The first day we visit them, they're a little hesitant," Officer McChesney says. "But once they get to know us, they give us hugs and are happy to see us when we stop by." Each month, officers also visit elementary-school classrooms to teach children about laws and show them that they don't need to be afraid of the police.

Asset 13

NEIGHBORHOOD BOUNDARIES

Neighbors take responsibility for monitoring and supervising children outside the home.

How Search Institute defines this asset . . .

For infants, toddlers, and preschoolers: Neighbors take responsibility for monitoring and supervising children's behavior as they begin to play and interact outside the home.

For elementary-age children: Neighbors take responsibility for monitoring children's behavior.

ALL CHILDREN

- Build Asset 4: Caring Neighborhood *before* creating neighborhood boundaries. When children feel known and cared for, boundaries are more effective.
- Be a role model. Show children how to behave appropriately by doing so yourself. Join parents and other adults in teaching children how to act.
- Each child is different and special. Don't compare children based on their behavior.
- Discuss boundaries with adults and children in your neighborhood. Make a list of rules and limits and distribute it.

Everyone may not agree on which boundaries are appropriate. Develop a way to discuss and resolve different opinions.

- Talk to the mayor or city council about developing a set of values for the community. Ask the local newspaper to donate space to publish the information.

- Invite police officers to a neighborhood gathering. Ask them to talk about how important it is for neighbors to keep an eye out for each other and to discuss the behaviors they see.

RESOURCE

National Civic League
1445 Market Street, Suite 300
Denver, CO 80202-1717
Telephone: (303) 571-4343
Web site: *www.ncl.org/*

The goal of the National Civic League (NCL) is to create communities that work for everyone. The NCL teaches adults, young people, and policy makers to work together to set neighborhood boundaries and to solve problems. Write, call, or visit their Web site for more information on their projects, including the Healthy Communities Program and the Youth Initiative Challenge.

INFANTS

- If you see a parent losing patience with an infant, express your concern. Offer to play with or hold the infant to give the parent a break.

- Schedule neighborhood gatherings at convenient times for families with children. Ask parents what times work best for them.

- Infants don't understand boundaries and limits. When an infant cries, she's not acting inappropriately, but letting people know she needs something. Talk about this with neighbors.

- Create neighborhood places where infants and parents can happily—and safely—spend time together.

- When infants are enjoying the outdoors, watch them carefully to make sure they aren't eating dirt, leaves, rocks, or other objects.

TODDLERS

- Show toddlers how to change their behavior when they act inappropriately. Say, "Please don't pull the puppy's tail. Pet him gently, like this."
- Fight the urge to laugh or smile when toddlers misbehave in ways that adults find funny.
- Neighborhood boundaries for toddlers should protect them but still give them freedom to have fun. Adults should be certain that toddlers have safe spaces to run and play—for example, in a fenced yard with a closed gate.
- Use humor to set boundaries. For example, a toddler may take off his socks and resist putting them back on. You might say, "You've taken off your socks. It looks like I get to wear them on my hands." This might help the toddler conclude, "No! Those socks are for *my* feet, not *your* hands!"
- Demonstrate what you say. When you want toddlers to put sidewalk chalk in a bucket, say so. Then do it with them to show what you mean.

PRESCHOOLERS

- Point out children's successes twice as often as their failures or mistakes.
- Be a spokesperson for the neighborhood. For example, when a preschooler curses, say, "We don't swear in our neighborhood. Please stop."
- Expect children to respect other children and the environment at neighborhood playgrounds and play areas.
- Tell parents in private about their preschooler's inappropriate behavior. Be nonjudgmental. Just say, "I wanted to let you know that Jenny hit the neighbor."

ELEMENTARY-AGE CHILDREN

- Let children know you've noticed when they act inappropriately. Tell them that you expect more of them.

- Set up a "neighborhood theater" for children in the area. Have them role-play situations and discuss appropriate ways to act. Give them a few ideas to get them started (two children with one ice-cream cone, an audience at a piano recital), then let them act out ideas of their own.
- Have children accept some consequences of their behavior. Don't always step in and rescue them, but don't abandon them, either. For example, if a child rides her bike across the neighbor's flower bed, don't immediately take care of the damage yourself. See if she can help plant new flowers.

ASSETS IN ACTION
Setting Clear Boundaries

Northfield, Minnesota, struggled with an umpire shortage for the community baseball association because of the foul language and inappropriate behavior of the adults in the stands. Parents and officials were also concerned that children would pick up these bad habits from the adults, so the association created a code of conduct based on the assets and printed it on business-size cards. Now, when someone at a game begins to act inappropriately, a designated person hands the offender a card. The card reads, "We appreciate your attendance. Our participants need your positive support and encouragement. Abusive behavior by players, coaches, umpires, or fans will not be tolerated. If your behavior continues, we will stop the game until you leave the premises."

In addition, the association wrote guidelines for behavior that are distributed to all players, coaches, parents, and umpires. Before a child can play baseball, the child and his or her parents must sign an asset-building agreement that spells out expectations for behavior and participation. The coaches also receive a one-page handout called "Developing a Coaching Philosophy" based on the assets.

Based on these changes, the association now has a waiting list of people wanting to be umpires.

Asset 14

ADULT ROLE MODELS

Children learn how to act and interact with others by watching, imitating, and modeling their parents, caregivers, and other adults. Adults set good examples for children.

How Search Institute defines this asset . . .

For infants, toddlers, preschoolers, and elementary-age children: Parents and other adults model positive, responsible behavior.

ALL CHILDREN

- Parents who are positive role models have a sense of purpose, which supports Asset 14: Adult Role Models and also builds Asset 39: Sense of Purpose in children. Parents can keep working toward all their personal dreams and goals, even if they need to slow their progress while they raise their children.
- Nurture the relationships children have with extended family members, teachers, and neighbors. Tell these adults how much you appreciate the role modeling they do.
- Be what you want children to be. If you believe that education is important, take a class or study something that builds your skills or interests. Share what you're learning with children.

INFANTS

- Talk to parents and caregivers about meeting the needs of infants immediately and consistently. Explain that doing this makes them adult role models.
- Give parents and caregivers a break from caring for an infant. Adult role models also need time to care for themselves.
- If you enjoy infants, spend a lot of time with them. An adult who's enthusiastic about babies is a great role model.
- Talk with first-time parents about how they're doing and support them as they learn.

TODDLERS

- Enjoy toddlers when they wear Daddy's shoes or want to carry a purse like Mommy. Play along with them as they imitate their first role models: their parents.
- Model how to behave when toddlers throw temper tantrums. Be calm and rational. Don't mimic or tease the toddler.
- Pretend play is a way for toddlers to experiment with acting grown-up. Have fun sipping imaginary tea when they serve you a cup. Admire the projects they make at their toy workbenches.
- Help children find positive role models on television and in books. Many toddlers like heroes such as Barney and Baby Bop, Elmo and Zoe from *Sesame Street*, the Teletubbies, and the baby in Helen Oxenbury's board books (*I Can, I Hear, I See,* and *I Touch*).

PRESCHOOLERS

- Talk with preschoolers about the characters they see on television. Say, "Do you think that person did the right thing? What would you choose to do?" Have conversations like this frequently.
- Let preschoolers dress like older children and adults they admire. Some want to style their hair in ponytails like the baby-sitter's. Others want to wear red socks like Uncle Matt.

- Think of yourself as a preschooler's superhero. Although preschoolers might prefer to dress like Superman or Superwoman, they're watching adults like yourself for cues on how to act.

- Help preschoolers think about the adults they admire. Continue to talk about the difference between positive and negative role models (children will need several years to learn this).

- Be clear about which superheroes are acceptable and which are not. If a preschooler is drawn to aggressive, overtly sexual, or violent superheroes, identify more acceptable superheroes who resolve problems or express feelings in positive ways.

- Use familiar characters as teachers. For example, using the main character from the book *Piggy Washes Up* by Carol Thompson (Cambridge, MA: Candlewick Press, 1989), say, "Piggy asks for help from an adult when he doesn't know what to do. You can be like Piggy and ask for help, too."

RESOURCE

Save the Children
1620 I Street NW, #202
Washington, DC 20006
Telephone: (202) 293-4170
Web site: *www.savethechildren.org*

Save the Children, which was started by 12-year-old Jason Dean Crowe, is a member of the International Save the Children Alliance, one of the world's largest partnerships working on behalf of children today. Their ongoing work includes a campaign to encourage adults to become mentors. To get involved, visit their Web site or call toll free: 1-877-Be-A-Mentor (1-877-232-6368).

ELEMENTARY-AGE CHILDREN

- Talk about the adult role models you had as a child and what you liked about them. Ask children to name admirable traits of the adults they know.

- Give children access to many kinds of adult role models—young, old, rich, poor, single, married, silly, or serious.

- Send for pictures and information about a child's favorite sports hero, author, artist, actor, or musician. Talk about things the child and her hero have in common and how they are different. Help children see that these heroes are ordinary people.

- Encourage children to make bulletin boards, posters, or scrapbooks about their favorite heroes. Together, visit the library and research the lives of these people. Talk about their strengths and weaknesses.

- Although children may seem more interested in movie or sports celebrities, their real adult role models are the adults around them. Help children meet adults who are good role models, and act like a role model worth following.

ASSETS IN ACTION
Modeling High Expectations

The Big Brothers Big Sisters of Delta County in Escanaba, Michigan, created an asset-building program that matches high school sophomores, juniors, and seniors with elementary-age children. Called High Five Mentoring℠, the program matches one teenager with one child. The pair gets together once a week to work on an assignment given by the younger child's teacher. Because boys are less likely to volunteer for mentoring programs, the agency recruits entire classes, not individual young people. The elementary-age children have improved their academic performance because of the program. Additionally, everyone involved—both the children and the teenagers—has had better school attendance, and the teen mentors have improved their attitudes about education, volunteering, and children in general.

Asset 15

POSITIVE PEER INTERACTION AND INFLUENCE

**Children spend time observing
and playing with children of varying ages.
As children grow, they spend time
with friends who act in responsible ways.**

How Search Institute defines this asset . . .

For infants and toddlers: Infants and toddlers observe siblings and other children interacting in positive ways. They have opportunities to interact with children of various ages.

For preschoolers: Preschoolers are encouraged to play and interact with other children in safe, well-supervised settings.

For elementary-age children: Children interact with other children who model responsible behavior and have opportunities to play and interact in safe, well-supervised settings.

ALL CHILDREN

- Observe how people around you interact. What are children seeing? What are they learning about how people treat each other?
- Find ways for children of all ages to have fun together. Teenagers can hold and rock babies. An older child might tell a story to a toddler.

INFANTS

- Respond to an infant's needs. This will help him learn to trust others.

- Surround an infant with siblings, friends, and adults who treat each other with respect and appreciate each other.

- Teach older siblings how to play safely and gently with a new baby. Show them simple ways to play, talk, and spend time with the infant.

- Give babies opportunities to be near other babies. Even though they don't play together, infants may watch each other, imitate each other, and communicate without words.

TODDLERS

- Expect toddlers to play alone, even when they're with other children. Children will slowly begin to interact with their peers when they're in preschool.

- Arrange for toddlers to play near other toddlers. Watch them carefully to make sure they're getting along. Caregivers can talk and share ideas while children play.

- Toddlers will hit, poke, bite, pull hair, and swipe other children's toys. This isn't because they're mean, but because they're trying to figure out their own space and what it means to share. Correct them gently and teach skills based on what you see.

- Keeping toddlers fed, dry, not over- or understimulated, and well rested will create a successful playtime. A toddler won't enjoy playing if she's uncomfortable.

- Create an interesting play area for toddlers. A sandbox with sand toys or a playroom with age-appropriate toys can be a lot of fun.

RESOURCE

Little Bean's Friend by John Wallace (New York: HarperCollins, 1996). When Little Bean loses her teddy bear, she meets Paul next door and has her first experience with friendship.

DID YOU KNOW?

Asset 11: Family Boundaries and Asset 15: Positive Peer Interaction and Influence are related. Researcher Gary Ladd found that a mother's style of discipline influences how the preschooler interacts with other children. Mothers who set limits and explain consequences have preschoolers who get along well with others. Children who have trouble with peers tend to have mothers who hit, yell, and threaten.

Source: Craig H. Hart, Gary W. Ladd, and Brant R. Burleson, "Children's Expectations of the Outcomes of Social Strategies: Relations with Sociometric Status and Maternal Disciplinary Styles." *Child Development* 61, no. 1 (1990).

PRESCHOOLERS

- Find playtime projects that teach preschoolers how to cooperate. For example, children can build a block city together. When preschoolers can't resolve their differences, step in and show them ways to settle problems.

- Hold a tea party for a preschooler and his favorite stuffed animals. Learn the name of each furry friend. Enjoy being with the child and his toys.

- Invite only one child over to play when a preschooler wants a friend to visit. More than two preschoolers playing in a home can lead to chaos.

- Don't panic when preschoolers say "I hate you" or "You're not my friend anymore" to a playmate. Preschoolers are learning how to express their feelings, and they often make up with others quickly—even if they've said they never will.

- Keep preschool playtimes with friends short. One or two hours is long enough.

- Children need to build friendships with people of all ages. Make friends with a preschooler and teach her how to be a friend. Ask questions like, "What are some things that friends do?"

ELEMENTARY-AGE CHILDREN

- Give children some independence when they're playing with friends, but check on them often to make sure they're safe.

- Ask a child and his friends if you can play with them for a few minutes. Toss a football. Make a beaded necklace. Tell funny stories.

- When children argue and disagree, let them find their own solutions. Step in to help only if you're concerned about the children's safety—for example, if a child starts to hit.

- Talk to children after they play with their friends. Ask questions like, "Did you have fun with your friends? What did you like best? What didn't you like?" Talk about some of the behaviors you saw. Discuss ways to smooth sticky situations.

- Children get more involved in friendships as they grow older. Get to know their friends. Find out who they like—and why.

- Talk about the friendships—and problems—you had when you were younger. For example, if you had trouble with a bully, tell a child about it. Sometimes this helps children open up.

- A lot of what children know about rules, beliefs, attitudes, and how to interact with other people comes from their friends. What are children learning? Talk with them and find out. For example, you might ask, "What does your friend do when she's mad? when she wants something? How well does your friend listen to her parents?"

Asset 16

APPROPRIATE EXPECTATIONS FOR GROWTH

Parents and other adults have realistic expectations for children's development and don't push beyond the child's own pace. Adults encourage children to do their best and develop their unique talents.

How Search Institute defines this asset . . .

For infants and toddlers: Parents have realistic expectations for children's development at this age. Parents encourage development without pushing children beyond their own pace.

For preschoolers and elementary-age children: Adults have realistic expectations for children's development at this age. Parents, caregivers, and other adults encourage children to achieve and develop their unique talents.

ALL CHILDREN

- Children develop at their own speed. Don't push them or hold them back. Be patient and let children do things when they're ready. Talk to a pediatrician, a teacher, or another specialist if you think a child is developing at a different rate from other children. (See pages 92 and 93 for some helpful resources on ages and stages of development.)
- A child is a whole person, with strengths and weaknesses. Don't use his differences to label him. For example, if a child

stutters, don't call him a stutterer. Share your concerns with a teacher, special-education professional, child-development specialist, or doctor and ask for ways to help the child.

RESOURCE

National Association for the Education of Young Children (NAEYC)
1509 16th Street NW
Washington, DC 20036
Telephone: (202) 232-8777
Fax: (202) 328-1846
Toll-free phone: 1-800-424-2460
Web site: *www.naeyc.org*

NAEYC helps groups and individuals promote healthy child development and constructive education for all young children. Anyone who wishes to act on behalf of children can become a member. NAEYC also publishes helpful newsletters and books, including *Developmentally Appropriate Practice in Early Childhood Programs,* edited by Sue Bredekamp and Carol Copple (revised edition, 1997), which is an excellent resource for childcare providers and others who spend time with young children.

* Pay attention to what children like. Do they enjoy music? reading? outdoor games? puzzles? Following their interests and passions helps children grow. Give them time to explore.
* Think of expectations as a helium balloon with a string attached. If the balloon loses too much air (expectations are low), it isn't fun anymore. If the balloon isn't attached to the child's wrist and floats away beyond reach (expectations are too high), it's frustrating for the child. Keep your expectations reasonable.
* Routines help children feel safe, protected, and free to explore. Children who aren't worried about when they'll eat or sleep can concentrate on learning new skills.

INFANTS

- When the infant starts rolling over, crawling, or sitting up, or reaches another milestone, celebrate! Show the infant how delighted and proud you are.

- Let infants take the lead in accomplishing milestones such as grasping, crawling, or walking on their own timetable. These milestones occur when the baby is physically developed enough to accomplish them. Don't push the baby to succeed at these tasks before she's ready—even if you know other babies who've mastered them earlier.

- Talk to older children about infants before a new baby arrives. Show children pictures of themselves as infants, visit a family with an infant, or visit the maternity ward at a hospital. This helps children understand what to expect from the new baby.

TODDLERS

- Marvel at toddlers' achievements. Encourage them when they're mastering new skills, such as climbing stairs while holding the railing, or learning new words. Say, "Wow! Listen to all the words you know!" Let your tone of voice show how excited you are about what they can do.

- Try to give toddlers extra time to practice new things. If a toddler wants to get dressed by himself, give him time to do this. Be patient as a toddler learns to do something new, and don't expect perfection. Criticism can hamper rather than help a toddler. Encouragement can deepen the child's interest.

- Let toddlers play with stimulating toys that stretch their abilities. Direct toddlers toward toys they like and away from toys that frustrate them.

- Challenge toddlers by having them help you find things they want or need. For example, when a toddler asks for juice, don't just give it to her. Open the oven and ask, "Is the juice in here?" When the toddler says no, say, "Show me where the juice is."

PRESCHOOLERS

- When you play with a preschooler, ask specific questions to stimulate the child's creativity. For example, if a preschooler says, "I'm the teacher. You listen to me," say, "Okay, but I need help. What do you want me to draw?"
- Mastering a skill can take time, so be patient and understand that setbacks will happen. For example, a toilet-trained child can have accidents now and then. Stay positive and don't punish the child.
- Praise a preschooler by suggesting he's acting like an older child. For example, you might say to a 4-year-old, "Thank you for picking up your toys. You're acting like a kindergartner!" However, never shame a child by comparing him to a younger child ("Stop grabbing! You're acting like a baby!"). Deal with the inappropriate behavior directly: "We don't grab what we want—what do we say?"

ELEMENTARY-AGE CHILDREN

- Teach children that sometimes things don't work out like we expect. Ask, "Did you learn anything from what happened?"
- Talk with a child about things that are difficult for her. Help her figure out how to break a big task down into manageable pieces. For example, help the child create a checklist of steps she'll need to take to complete an assignment or reach a goal. The child can use this to track her progress and decide what to do next.
- Involve children in clubs and activities that fit their abilities and encourage them to develop other skills also. Introduce them to people who'll challenge them to grow. Find stimulating environments that match children's abilities and personalities.
- Have children compare themselves to . . . themselves. How is the child doing now compared to the past? Is he finding new challenges? Is he improving?
- Model high expectations for yourself. Tell a child about a goal or dream you're striving toward and what's happened along the way.

MORE IDEAS FOR BUILDING THE BOUNDARIES AND EXPECTATIONS ASSETS

IDEAS FOR PARENTS

• Learn as much as you can about your child's personality and developmental needs. For example, if your daughter is a "spirited child" (a term used by author Mary Sheedy Kurcinka), you'll understand why she throws temper tantrums when you cut her toast into triangles instead of circles.

RESOURCE

Raising Your Spirited Child by Mary Sheedy Kurcinka (New York: HarperCollins, 1992) talks about children's challenging personality traits in a positive way and gives readers specific tools to deal with these traits.

• Balance boundaries and support. Children need to know limits (and have them upheld consistently), and they need to know they're loved.

• Expect messy mealtimes for the first few years of a child's life. Be patient when children are learning how to behave at the table.

• If you want your children to do something, do it yourself, too. For example, if you want your children to floss their teeth each day, put a star on the calendar every day everyone does this. After a few weeks or a month of success, celebrate by going out for a movie or having a picnic in the park.

• Be firm about giving prescription medicine to your children. If they strongly resist, ask your pediatrician for some ways to make things easier. A doctor can usually give you ideas that have worked for other parents.

- Learn about your children's classroom and school boundaries. Talk to teachers and administrators if you aren't sure what these rules are or you have questions.
- Use humor and be creative in enforcing boundaries. For example, say, "If the table isn't cleared off before suppertime, we'll have to hold our plates in our hands and eat standing up!" (Make sure you keep your promise if the child doesn't cooperate.)

IDEAS FOR CHILDCARE PROVIDERS

- Make a clear, simple, and short list of boundaries for young children. If possible, try to phrase the rules in a positive way. For example: "Be helpful. Use your inside voice. Be kind to others."
- Take a "childcare family photo" each year. Arrange for a professional photographer, a parent, or a volunteer to take a photo of the entire group, including caregivers. This keepsake photograph can help children remember special people at the childcare center. (Be sure to include a card with everyone's names.)
- If you'll be away from the childcare setting for an extended period of time, arrange for a substitute and let parents know as far in advance as possible. Switching caregivers can be upsetting to a young child when children and parents don't know what to expect.
- Offer at least one conference each year to talk with parents about their child's development. This is a great opportunity to develop a relationship with parents and share the child's triumphs and struggles in your care.
- Recruit volunteers who can be positive role models for children. Volunteers might be senior citizens, teenagers from the local high school, college students, or employees from a nearby business.

IDEAS FOR EDUCATORS

- Talk to parents about boundaries. Tell them about the school and classroom boundaries.

- If possible, send a list of classroom rules to your students' parents before the school year begins. Let parents know what will happen if a child breaks a rule. Ask parents to support the rules and talk to their children about them.

- Supervise students at all times—in the classroom, at recess, in the cafeteria, and in the halls. If you can't be present, find another responsible adult to keep watch.

- Develop a routine so students know what to expect each day. Send a copy of your weekly schedule home with each student so parents know what happens when.

- Talk about positive role models in literature, history, science, and other subjects. Create lessons that teach students about each person's strengths and weaknesses.

- Assign group projects so children can learn to work together and build relationships with others. Change the groups often so children can work with many of their classmates.

IDEAS FOR HEALTH-CARE PROFESSIONALS

- Teach health-care staff members and volunteers about the 40 developmental assets. Explain that they build Asset 3: Other Adult Relationships and Asset 14: Adult Role Models when they set an example for children.

- Teach parents some basic facts about child development. Remind them that each child develops at a different pace. If they're concerned about their child, listen to their concerns and answer their questions.

- Ask parents to schedule appointments when their children are most alert. An examination can be more difficult if a child has skipped a meal or a nap.

- Provide phone numbers for after-hour services and consultations. Be clear about what parents can expect at these times.

- Let children know what to expect during physical examinations and procedures. Don't surprise children with sudden movements or shots. Talk to children and parents about what to expect during the next visit. Explain everything carefully, in language they can understand.

IDEAS FOR CONGREGATIONAL LEADERS

- Expect children to learn more about your faith tradition. Give them thought-provoking activities to spark their interest.
- Help children connect with each other outside the congregation. With parents' permission, publish a directory including children's names and the names of their parents, addresses, and phone numbers. Give a copy of this directory to each family.
- Post rules in all religious education rooms. Be clear about the consequences children can expect if they don't follow the rules.
- Create a code of conduct for religious services. What do you expect from children and infants at services? Discuss this with members of your congregation. Don't make the rules discouraging to families with young children. Expect some level of noise, talking, and moving around. Make sure your congregation is welcoming to families with children.

ASSETS IN ACTION
Faith Partners

St. Luke Presbyterian Church in Minnetonka, Minnesota, launched a faith partners program that matches interested adults and children. Each year about 60 to 70 people participate. The program's goal is to form informal relationships. Many partners seek each other out before religious services and sit together, and talk afterward. In addition, the congregation recognizes two children in the congregation as "stars of the week." Worship bulletins feature short biographical sketches of each child, and the children are introduced to the congregation during the service.

IDEAS FOR EMPLOYERS

- Bring volunteer opportunities to your employees. Invite a representative from a service organization to come to your workplace, pass out information, and answer questions.
- When can employees bring children to work? How long can children stay? Outline these policies in a staff handbook.
- Invite parents in your company to form a parent network. Have regular meetings to talk about the 40 developmental assets.
- Offer workshops to help parents learn how to set appropriate boundaries and enforce them consistently.
- Recognize adult role models in your company who work with young people. Write about them in your company newsletter. Send a press release about them to your community newspaper.

IDEAS FOR LIBRARIANS

- Form a task force of adults and children to create a clear set of boundaries and consequences for your library.
- Post the library's boundaries and consequences. Make copies for patrons to take with them.
- Train all librarians, volunteers, and library staff about the 40 developmental assets. Emphasize how each person is an adult role model.
- Educate the staff on how to be respectful and supportive while enforcing boundaries. Role-play possible situations in a staff training session.
- Set up storytimes when caring adults read stories to children. Schedule different storytimes for different age groups.

IDEAS FOR COMMUNITY LEADERS

- Bring school administrators together to compare and discuss their school boundaries. Help them create boundaries that are consistent.
- Build strong neighborhood groups and associations so residents can first build a caring neighborhood (Asset 4) and then create neighborhood boundaries (Asset 13).

- Keep the developmental needs of children in mind when creating, developing, or remodeling public places. Make these places child-friendly.

- Mix people of different ages in the community. For example, suggest developing childcare centers and after-school programs near senior citizen housing.

- Sponsor a community awards night to recognize children, teenagers, and adults who are positive role models. Publish an entry form in a community paper for individuals to nominate others. Distribute these forms at schools, childcare settings, senior centers, and elsewhere.

We encourage you to photocopy this page (set the image size at 125 percent), cut out the "Ideas for Children," and share them with a child you know.

IDEAS FOR CHILDREN:
BUILD YOUR OWN BOUNDARIES
AND EXPECTATIONS ASSETS

- Learn the rules at home, at your school, and in your neighborhood. Find out what will happen if you break a rule.

- After you learn the rules, follow them. If you don't like the rules, talk with adults about how to make the rules more fair.

- Learn more about the adults who are important to you. Ask them questions and find out what they like to do.

- Make friends with people who do things you admire and respect. They'll help bring out the best in you.

- Ask questions about things you don't understand. Try new things. Find ways to challenge yourself.

THE CONSTRUCTIVE
USE OF TIME ASSETS

Most children don't decide how they spend their time—they need adults to choose and create activities for them. With encouragement and support from parents and other caring people, children can enjoy fun, meaningful activities that help them become caring, creative, confident adults.

The constructive use of time category includes four developmental assets for children from birth through age 11:

The Constructive Use of Time Assets

Asset 17: Creative Activities

Asset 18: Out-of-Home Activities

Asset 19: Religious Community

Asset 20: Positive, Supervised Time at Home

When Search Institute surveyed 6th graders, they found that children experience some of the constructive use of time assets more than others. Here are the percentages of these children who reported each of the assets in their lives:*

Asset 17: Creative Activities	**23%**
Asset 18: Youth Programs	**57%**
Asset 19: Religious Community	**72%**
Asset 20: Time at Home	**57%**

---

*Some of the asset names in the survey of 6th graders are different from those relating to younger children. The survey's asset names are the names that apply to older children and teens. The asset names in *What Young Children Need to Succeed* take into account developmental and situational differences of young children. See pages 3–5 for further information about asset language.

Asset 17

CREATIVE ACTIVITIES

> **Parents expose all children to music, art, or other creative activities. As they mature, children begin to participate in these activities regularly.**

How Search Institute defines this asset . . .

For infants: Parents expose infants to music, art, or other creative aspects of the environment each day.

For toddlers: Parents expose toddlers to music, art, or other creative age-appropriate activities each day.

For preschoolers: Preschoolers participate in music, art, dramatic play, or other creative activities each day.

For elementary-age children: Children participate in music, art, drama, or other creative activities for at least three hours a week at home and elsewhere.

ALL CHILDREN

- Play music when children are around. Switch between soothing music (such as lullabies and light jazz), stimulating music (such as classical), and lively music (such as country and rock).
- Dance with a child to all kinds of music. Let him move with the music and create his own dance.

- Display children's art at work, at home, in libraries—and anywhere else. Ask a neighborhood business (such as a grocery store or car dealership) to sponsor a children's art exhibit in their building.

RESOURCE

Coming Up Taller
Web site: *www.cominguptaller.org/*

Visit this Web site to learn more about community arts and humanities programs for children and what the President's Committee on the Arts and Humanities is doing to advance them. Read program profiles, find out about current initiatives, and connect to other sources of information.

INFANTS

- Infants explore the world through taste and touch. Give them safe, age-appropriate toys and rattles to play with.
- Introduce an older infant to puppets. Give each puppet a name and create a special voice for it.
- Show infants colors and shapes. Black-and-white high-contrast items fascinate many infants. Add more colors and shapes as the infant grows. Be alert to when the infant gets tired or her attention wanes, which she'll show by looking away. When this happens, don't push the baby to keep interacting with the shapes.
- Sing to infants. They don't care if you can carry a tune—they just enjoy hearing your voice.

TODDLERS

- Give toddlers toys that spark their imagination. Let them experiment with wooden blocks, large Legos, thick crayons and large pieces of paper, and geometric shapes.
- Take toddlers to petting zoos, sculpture gardens, and hands-on museums where they can move freely and explore.

- Let toddlers experience music. This can be as simple as turning on the radio. Give toddlers the chance to hear many different instruments, rhythms, and tones.
- Anticipate messes. Give toddlers freedom to play with nontoxic finger paints (or even pudding) within a specific area (like in an empty bathtub or on a clean sidewalk on a sunny afternoon). Keep in mind that setup and cleanup may take longer than the activity itself.
- Give toddlers simple instruments or household items (like pots and pans) to create their own music. Applaud their concerts and their creativity.
- For mess-free creativity, let toddlers paint with paint brushes and water on sidewalks, fences, and other outdoor "canvases."

PRESCHOOLERS

- Keep a variety of materials on hand for preschoolers' art projects: sand, leaves, sticks, clay, cardboard boxes, glue or paste, egg cartons, and so on. Make masterpieces together.
- Visit children's museums, especially those with hands-on exhibits. Allow preschoolers plenty of time to learn and explore.
- When children are listening to music, give them crayons and paper. Ask them to draw what they see in their imagination.
- Give preschoolers puppets and simple costumes. Say, "Can you use these things to tell a story?" Attend their theatrical performances.
- Teach children simple music concepts. For example, show them what a note looks like. Talk about rhythm and show them how to clap to a musical beat.
- Preschoolers can play along with music with simple rhythm instruments (such as cymbals, tambourines, triangles, rain shakers, castanets, jingle taps, tick-tock blocks, and drums). Or create instruments out of spoons, sealed bags or boxes filled with rice or dry beans, and pots and pans.

DID YOU KNOW?

The Goals 2000: Educate America Act, passed in 1994, makes the arts an important part of education for children of all ages. According to *The National Standards for Art Education*, studying and practicing music, theater and dance, and the visual arts can teach children to:

- understand past and present human experiences
- learn to adapt to and respect the way other people think, work, and express themselves
- find ways to solve problems creatively
- make decisions when there are no standard answers
- communicate their thoughts and feelings in many different ways.

Source: *The National Standards for Art Education*, Arts Standards Project, directed by John J. Mahlmann (Reston, VA: Music Educators National Conference, 1994).

ELEMENTARY-AGE CHILDREN

- Introduce children to poetry. They might enjoy the work of Joanna Cole, Tomie dePaola, Myra Cohn Livingston, A.A. Milne, Naomi Shihab Nye, Shel Silverstein, Robert Louis Stevenson, or Jane Yolen. Have children make up their own poems, rhymes, and haiku.

- Talk to children about what instrument they might like to play: piano, guitar, a band instrument, or an orchestral instrument. Provide them with lessons or investigate what's available at school or in the community at low or no cost.

- Introduce children to the work of famous artists such as Rembrandt, Grandma Moses, Claude Monet, Claude Gellée, Mary Cassatt, Pablo Picasso, Sesshu, and the Yoruba of Nigeria. Teach them a few facts about these artists' lives.

- Ask children which arts they enjoy most at school—do they prefer music, drawing, theater, or dance? Help them develop their interests outside of school. For example, enroll children in community programs or parks and recreation department activities.

- Attend local concerts, art exhibits, and plays. Some communities sponsor free events in parks in the summer or over school breaks.

- Watch for children's illustrators, authors, and musicians who may visit your community. Take children to meet these people.

- If you have access to the Internet, visit a children's museum on the Web together and explore various exhibits. Some interesting places to visit include the Children's Museum of Memphis *(www.cmom.com)*, the Long Island Children's Museum *(www.licm.org/)*, and the Hands On Children's Museum *(www.hocm.org)*. If you don't have a computer, you and a child may be able to access the Internet at a local library.

- Experiment with different forms of art: sculpting, watercolor painting, papier-mâché, and so on. Do several projects using the same method so children can improve their skills.

ASSETS IN ACTION
A Hallway of Creativity

At Tuttle Elementary School in Minneapolis, Minnesota, children painted a mural in the school's entrance hallway. Each grade created one panel of the mural. When the mural was unveiled at a ceremony in November of 1998, children sang and performed choreographed dances to add to the festive and creative atmosphere.

Asset 18

OUT-OF-HOME ACTIVITIES

Parents expose children to appropriate stimulating activities with the child's needs in mind. Elementary-age children regularly participate in sports, clubs, or other community programs.

How Search Institute defines this asset . . .

For infants and toddlers: Parents expose children to limited but stimulating situations outside the home. The family keeps children's needs in mind when attending events.

For preschoolers: Preschoolers interact in stimulating ways with children outside the family. The family keeps preschoolers' needs in mind when attending events.

For elementary-age children: Children spend one hour or more each week in extracurricular school activities or structured community programs.

ALL CHILDREN

- Look for activities that are fun for children. Programs that push children to excel often aren't enjoyable—and can be harmful.
- Introduce children to animals. Take them to zoos and farms, on nature walks, and to visit neighbors who have pets. Teach children to approach neighborhood pets cautiously and ask the owner for permission to touch or play with the pet.

- Routines are important for children. Make sure that children's activities and schedules are planned and predictable.

RESOURCE

Boys & Girls Clubs of America
1230 West Peachtree Street NW
Atlanta, GA 30309
Telephone: (404) 815-5700
Web site: *www.boysandgirlsclub.org/*

Boys & Girls Clubs offer fun and educational activities for kids of all ages. Their mission is to help children realize their full potential as productive, responsible, and caring people. Call, write, or visit the Web site to find a club in your area.

Head Start and Early Head Start

Many communities have Head Start and Early Head Start programs. The mission of both organizations is to support the healthy development of infants, toddlers, and preschoolers by providing services for education, socio-emotional development, physical and mental health, and nutrition for children in low-income families. The cornerstone of these programs is parent and community involvement. If you can't find a Head Start or an Early Head Start program in your community, visit the Web site of the Early Head Start National Resource Center (EHSNRC) at *www.ehsnrc.org/*. The site has a link to Head Start's national home page.

INFANTS

- Make sure that childcare settings provide a warm, nurturing environment for infants, along with age-appropriate toys. Do caregivers meet infants' needs? Are infants happy, fed, and dry? Do they get a balance of activities and rest? If you have any concerns, talk to the director or supervisor of the center.
- Take an infant on short trips outside. Put her in a stroller and take her around the block or to a neighborhood park.

- Give infants a change of scene now and then. Move the rocking chair to a different room. Take a walk outside.
- Bring infants along on everyday outings to the grocery store or the mall. If possible, schedule these errands when the infant is fed and rested. Cut a trip short if it isn't going well for the baby.
- When you go places with an infant, put the infant first and the event second. If the infant gets restless or starts to cry, it's time to leave.

TODDLERS

- Visits to places like the grocery store can be lots of fun. Point out different colors, shapes, and sizes of food. Show toddlers a purple eggplant and a red cabbage. Compare big and small cans.
- Show toddlers different ways to get around. Take a short trip on a city bus or subway. Ride a wagon. Go on a hayride.
- Every day, spend time outdoors with a toddler—for example, jump in puddles during a spring shower. Watch toddlers closely whenever they're outside.
- Go to a parade. Talk about what you see and hear.

PRESCHOOLERS

- Visit interesting buildings together. Tour a barn, skyscraper, fire station, or bakery.
- Preschoolers can learn about the world at ordinary places (such as stores and car washes). Make these trips interesting. Asking questions—and watching the adults around them—can teach children a lot.
- Find structured activities for preschoolers to enjoy outside the home. For some children, this might be a childcare setting or a preschool. A preschool art class or beginning ballet or swimming lessons might work for others. For some free or low-cost options, check with your local parks and recreation department or community education center.

ELEMENTARY-AGE CHILDREN

- Let children experiment with different activities they like. Learn more about the options that are available in your area. Many programs are free or inexpensive, and scholarships are sometimes available.

- If children's sports leagues focus on competition, start some "fun" teams for kids. Make sure that kids on all teams have fun by learning about cooperation and sportsmanship. Thank coaches who praise and support every child on the team.

- Enroll children in activities that teach children skills while giving them interesting, well-rounded experiences. For example, scouting helps children build many of the 40 assets.

 DID YOU KNOW?

Studies show that children who participate in quality after-school programs get along better with others, have higher grades and self-esteem, and behave better in school than children who don't participate in these programs. Teachers and principals report that children in after-school programs handle conflicts effectively and enjoy reading for pleasure.

Source: "Fact Sheet on School-Age Children's Out-of-School Time," National Institute on Out-of-School Time (Wellesley, MA: Center for Research on Women, Wellesley College, 1998).

- Keep an eye on children's schedules. There should be more to a child's life than organized activities. Children also need family time, homework time, playtime, and quiet time.

- Help children make choices about what they'd like to do. Ask, "What are some good things about this activity? What are some bad things?" Talk with children about ways to select activities that are right for them.

- Involve children in team activities (such as a team sport or a choir) as well as individual ones (such as piano lessons or karate).

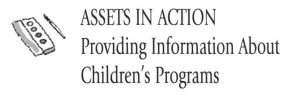

ASSETS IN ACTION
Providing Information About
Children's Programs

In Tennessee, 13 counties worked together to create a resource directory of service organizations. Each group that served children, youth, and families had a short description in the directory, and all the organizations listed set up booths at an informational fair. Area residents came to the fair to learn more about what each group offered and to pick up a free copy of the resource directory.

Asset 19

RELIGIOUS COMMUNITY

**Parents make religious programs
a regular part of family life.**

How Search Institute defines this asset . . .

For infants, toddlers, and preschoolers: The family regularly attends religious programs or services while keeping children's needs in mind.

For elementary-age children: The family attends religious programs or services for at least one hour per week.

ALL CHILDREN

- Build community within a congregation. Meet and get to know families with children. Develop congregational activities or groups especially for families with young children.
- Family religious traditions are an important way to help children form a lifelong connection to their faith. For example, some families light candles. Others eat special foods. If families don't have their own religious celebrations, talk about some rituals they might like to try.
- Go out of your way to learn the names of children and their parents in the congregation. Welcome these families when they attend services.

- Does your congregation have a library? If so, ask for donations of children's books that talk about your faith traditions. If not, talk to other members of the congregation about starting a library.
- Some congregations offer contemporary religious services especially for families. These services often include stories or lively songs that children enjoy. Consider attending these services, if they're offered by your congregation or by another area congregation that shares your faith. If this isn't an option, talk to a congregational leader about scheduling a contemporary service as a special event.

RESOURCE

Building Assets in Congregations by Eugene C. Roehlkepartain (Minneapolis: Search Institute, 1998) tells you everything you need to know to create an asset-building congregation, including program tips, reproducible bulletin inserts, and a planning guide.

INFANTS

- Check to see if infants are really welcome at religious services—you'll be able to tell by how people react to babies nearby. Some congregations provide nurseries, while others have "crying rooms" where caregivers can take infants who fuss during a religious service. Ask a congregational leader what kind of facilities are available.
- Talk with parents of infants about your faith upbringing. Share some things you hope the infant will learn.
- Watch an infant's tolerance for religious services and other religious events. Put the infant's needs first. For example, if an infant's cries drown out the service, take the baby to a quiet place to calm him.

TODDLERS

- Put toddlers in congregational nurseries or supervised toddler rooms during religious services. Don't expect toddlers to sit still for more than a few minutes during a religious service. If toddlers do come to services, give them books or favorite quiet activities.
- Plan extra time after a religious service to let a toddler give you a tour of the congregation's facilities.
- Talk with toddlers about the animals that appear in your faith tradition's stories. Mimic the different sounds the animals make.
- Find out how many toddlers are in your congregation. Learn their names. Make friends with them.
- Volunteer to play with toddlers in your congregation's nursery during religious services.
- Introduce simple words from your faith tradition. For example, you might say, "We *pray* as part of our faith. Do you know what *praying* is?" Help the child learn what your faith is all about.

PRESCHOOLERS

- Talk about aspects of your faith that a young child may enjoy, such as holiday celebrations, songs, special foods, and candles. Find ways for families to use these in their homes. For example, tape-record some of your faith's children's music and give the tapes to families.
- Create an activity bag of quiet toys a preschooler can play with during religious services.
- Expect children to ask questions about religion. Give simple explanations they can understand. At times, ask children questions about your faith tradition to find out what they're thinking.

ELEMENTARY-AGE CHILDREN

- Help children build relationships outside of religious services. For example, have a child invite a friend from the congregation over for dinner or playtime.

- As they grow older, children will be able to sit quietly for longer periods of time. Notice when children behave appropriately during religious services and tell them that you appreciate it. If a child continues to struggle with this, give her something to keep her occupied—she might look at or read a book, for example.

- Enroll children in your congregation's religious education classes to teach them more about the faith tradition. Help them get to know their classmates. Children will be more willing to attend services if they know they'll see friends there.

- When children visit friends or relatives who attend different congregations, have children attend services with them. Talk about the experience afterward. What was different? What was the same?

- Some children are raised in an interfaith family. Some parents choose to raise a child in one faith tradition. Others keep strong ties to both faith traditions. Still others make different choices with this issue. Whatever decision parents make, help children understand and appreciate both traditions. Talk to children about their religious questions.

ASSETS IN ACTION
Offering Worthwhile Activities

Temple Emanu-El in Dallas, Texas, examines its programming from a developmental perspective. "I think about how I can build bridges across the age groups," says Judi Ratner, the synagogue's youth director. Program leaders offer fun, meaningful activities for 1st- to 5th-graders three times a year "to create fellowship and a sense of continuity," Ratner says. Program leaders ask what they want 1st graders to be like when they graduate from high school, then plan the program with that focus. Ratner says forming a sense of community for children in the temple is important because many attend different schools.

Asset 20

POSITIVE, SUPERVISED TIME AT HOME

Parents ensure appropriate supervision of their children. Parents and children spend most evenings and weekends together at home in predictable, enjoyable routines.

How Search Institute defines this asset . . .

For infants and toddlers: Parents supervise children at all times and provide predictable, enjoyable routines at home.

For preschoolers: Preschoolers are supervised by an adult at all times. Preschoolers spend most evenings and weekends at home with their parents in predictable, enjoyable routines.

For elementary-age children: Children spend most evenings and weekends at home with their parents in predictable, enjoyable routines.

ALL CHILDREN

- Children thrive on a regular schedule. When children know what to expect, they can focus their energy on learning and growing.
- One of the best gifts you can give to a child is your undivided attention. Give it as often as you can.

- Plan family adventures. Visit a nearby lake and throw pebbles in the water. Step outside on a rainy day and examine the worms. Take a walk and point out different colors and shapes you see.

- Make sure adult family members spend plenty of time at home. Adults need time to themselves *and* a chance to get out. But it can be hard on children when they either spend too much time at home without their parents or the family spends too much time away from home.

- Children and adults can benefit from spending quiet time together. Do simple activities: appreciate a fresh snowfall, watch birds at a bird feeder, or curl up together to listen to music or a book on tape.

- Record favorite family songs on an audiocassette or CD. Play the recording in the car and sing along.

- Limit children's "screen time"—the time they spend watching television, playing video games, or using the computer. Be a good role model by talking, reading, and spending time with people instead of watching television.

INFANTS

- Try to spend as much time as possible at home with an infant. Make the infant's home a comforting, soothing place. Provide stimulating, interesting activities regularly to encourage children to learn.

- The home is the infant's primary world. Emphasize interesting sounds (by singing and playing music), tastes (especially as infants begin to eat solid food), sights, touches, and smells. For example, carry an infant on a tour of your home, or look at all the mirrors together.

- Notice your mood as you spend time with an infant. Do you feel calm and comfortable? If not, figure out what's bothering you. Infants can pick up on adults' feelings, so take a moment to relax.

- Play games with an infant. Pretend you're an airplane and the baby is the pilot. Get on the floor and wiggle toys in front of the baby to see what she's interested in.

- Just relax with an infant in your lap. Many babies like doing this for a long time.

TODDLERS

- Create unique rituals. For example, one dad always gave his croutons (one by one) to his toddler whenever the family ate salad. The ritual lasted until the child was a teenager.
- Set up a spot where a toddler can play near an adult who's doing chores. For example, pull out plastic containers for a toddler to bang around while an adult cooks. Or give a toddler a towel so he can "help" clean the bathroom.

 DID YOU KNOW?

Looking for a fun family activity? You don't have to turn on the television. Consider these facts:

- Number of minutes per week that the average American child ages 2–11 watches television: 1,197
- Number of minutes per week that parents spend in meaningful conversation with their children: 38.5
- Number of videos rented daily in the U.S.: 6 million
- Number of public library items checked out daily: 3 million

During National TV-Turnoff Week (the last week in April each year), people leave their televisions off and learn that life can be more constructive, rewarding, healthy—even informed—with more time and less TV. To get involved in this and other programs (and learn interesting facts like the ones listed here), contact TV-Free America, 1611 Connecticut Avenue NW, Suite 3A, Washington, DC 20009; telephone: (202) 887-0436; Web site: *www.tvfa.org.*

- Play the chasing game. Let the toddler run in a specific area as you try to catch her. (Remove all possible hazards beforehand.)

Take your time in catching the toddler. Toddlers also like easy games of hide and seek. They love to be found, and they love to find you.

- Make daily rituals fun. For example, when toddlers refuse to take a bath, say, "Let's take a new kind of bath." Then give toddlers a choice: a fast or slow bath, a deep or shallow bath (with adult supervision), a silly or serious bath, a bath with ducks or boats. Remember that toddlers' occasional negativity is part of their natural development. Be patient as toddlers start to understand and explore their separateness.

RESOURCE

Simple Fun for Busy People by Gary Krane, Ph.D. (Berkeley, CA: Conari Press, 1998), shows families hundreds of physical and mental games that can be played almost anywhere and anytime.

PRESCHOOLERS

- Create fun family times when bad weather forces everyone indoors. Following a heavy snowfall, fill the bathtub with snow and make snow sculptures. After a thunderstorm that takes out the electricity, pretend to be pioneers who have to do things the "old-fashioned way."
- Schedule quiet time for preschoolers who've outgrown naps. During quiet time they can draw, look at books, put stuffed animals down for a nap, or do other solitary activities.
- Make mealtimes fun. Tell jokes. Eat the meal backward, starting with dessert and ending with salad. Dress in costumes once in awhile. Have every family member tell one thing that happened that day.
- Plan a family treasure hunt through the home. Create maps and clues. The treasure might be a special note or a cartoon for each family member, hidden in a box.
- Create different worlds where preschoolers can play. Throwing a tablecloth over a chair or painting a large box to look like a spaceship helps spark a preschooler's imagination.

ELEMENTARY-AGE CHILDREN

- Create a jar of boredom busters. Name free activities family members could enjoy doing together. ("Take the neighbor's dog for a walk." "Write a book." "Tour a junk yard.") Write each suggestion on a small slip of paper and put all the slips in a jar. When the boredom blues hit, pull an activity out of the jar and give it a try.

- Take a family vacation from chores. Declare a weekend day as "no chores or errands day." Hang out together and do fun things. Let the unmade beds, dirty laundry, and dishes piled in the sink wait a day.

- Surprise a child by taking her out for an unexpected breakfast, movie, or ice-cream cone—just the two of you.

- Hang a monthly family calendar at children's eye level. Have a child stick a star on each night when everyone in the family is home. Aim to be home together at least three or four nights a week.

- On Sundays, have a comic-strip reading ritual. Read the comics together and vote for the funniest one. Let family members clip their favorites and hang them in a special place.

- Give children some time to themselves each day. If children have trouble getting used to this, suggest some activities in advance so they have something to do.

- Have a family "cave day." Turn off the ringer on the phone. Don't answer the door. Keep all curtains and blinds drawn. Unplug the television. Pretend you live in a cave and focus on the people in your home instead of things.

MORE IDEAS FOR BUILDING THE CONSTRUCTIVE USE OF TIME ASSETS

IDEAS FOR PARENTS

- Give children the chance to do art activities whenever they choose. Have lots of paper, crayons, markers, paints, and other inexpensive art supplies on hand, stored where children can easily reach them.
- Ask children what arts activities and programs they'd like to try. Sign them up, if possible.
- Limit the number of activities children can participate in. Help children set priorities and do the things they enjoy most. If they seem overwhelmed, work together to choose which activities to cut.

ASSETS IN ACTION
Outlining the Assets

In one family, a mother of three children (ages 4, 6, and 8) wanted to "outline" assets for her children. She had her children lie down on butcher paper, then drew outlines of their bodies. The children also made an outline of their mom, and the family taped all the outlines to the wall. Each day for two weeks, the mother and her children wrote and drew words and pictures about their assets on their outlines. Among the assets they illustrated were Asset 1: Family Support (hearts), Asset 17: Creative Activities (crayons), and Asset 25: Reading for Pleasure (books).

- Find a congregation that makes you feel comfortable and welcomes children.
- Make family fun a top priority. Hold a family meeting where you plan and schedule some activities you'll do together.
- Play all kinds of music in your home.

IDEAS FOR CHILDCARE PROVIDERS

- Give childcare staff members plenty of time to develop fun, age-appropriate art projects for children. Encourage them to find ideas at the library or in the center's resource materials.
- Once or twice a year, plan a picnic or party at a convenient time for families. Some family members don't get a chance to meet other people during drop-off and pick-up times.
- Schedule daytime programs as far in advance as possible so parents can attend. Some childcare settings give parents an activity calendar that includes all the special events planned for the coming year.
- Be sensitive to parents' schedules and spread activities throughout the year. Help parents create evening routines for children by limiting after-hours activities.
- Support children when they get excited about a religious holiday. You might say, "I can see that you're really looking forward to that special day." Be sensitive to children whose families celebrate more, fewer, or different religious holidays than most of the children in your care, or no religious holidays at all.
- Display children's artwork on walls, doors, and bulletin boards throughout the childcare facility.
- Create a list of free, fun ideas that families can do at home together. Give copies of this list to parents.

IDEAS FOR EDUCATORS

- Find creative art projects that challenge children's skills and stretch their imagination. For example, 2nd graders can learn about portrait painting, then do self-portraits or paintings of their friends. Expose children to the work of artists from many cultures, from the familiar classics to unusual modern pieces. Talk with children about what they like and what they don't like.

RESOURCE

Children's Art Foundation
P.O. Box 83
Santa Cruz, CA 95063
Telephone: (408) 426-5557
Web site: *www.stonesoup.com*

This organization works with individuals, schools, libraries, and other child-based organizations to encourage children to develop their artistic and literacy potential. It also publishes *Stone Soup,* a magazine by young writers and artists.

- If you coach or lead an after-school activity, use practice time to build assets. Give children a chance to develop skills, create relationships, and have fun.
- Avoid scheduling teacher conferences and other school activities on religious holidays. Learn what these holidays are for the various faith traditions that are part of your community.
- Create fun homework assignments that involve both children and the important adults in their lives. For example, children can give parents a questionnaire about their hobbies, interview a grandparent or an older adult, or list all the pets the family's had.
- Many parents are overwhelmed with activities during the last few weeks of the year. Spread programs and activities over the entire school year.

IDEAS FOR HEALTH-CARE PROFESSIONALS

- Provide constructive and safe activities for children in waiting areas. Create notebooks for parents that include information about asset building, your community's asset-building programs, phone numbers and calendars, and newsletters with information on community activities.

- Be sensitive to patients' schedules. If you're running behind, apologize for the wait. If you find yourself consistently running late, brainstorm with staff members to find ways to improve.

- Use the time you have with patients to help them feel good about themselves and the health-care center. For example, find out about patients' health habits and affirm the smart health choices they're making.

- Display children's artwork in your facilities. Some hospitals and clinics have local children's artwork framed and hung in the lobby.

- Suggest that families start a regular "family night" or "family day." (Some families do this weekly, others monthly.) Recommend activities and projects that families can do together.

- Children who are hospitalized or in long-term care can participate in constructive activities, too. Help these children express themselves creatively. Find ways for them to get involved in adaptive sports, scouting, or other group projects.

IDEAS FOR CONGREGATIONAL LEADERS

- Work with area schools to create a family night when no meetings or activities are scheduled.

- Teach children songs from your faith tradition. Make singing even more fun by creating actions to go along with the words.

- Plan special summer activities for children. Ask parents to suggest some things their children might enjoy.

- Perform a congregational play or musical each year. Write or adapt a script so family members of all ages can get involved. For example, children can direct, act, make scenery, and provide music.

- Create a "crying room" where parents can take young children during religious services. This may be a room with windows into the worship area, or a room with speakers connected to the public address system so parents can hear what's happening.

- Have a family potluck before or after congregational meetings. Arrange for adults to care for children during meetings so parents don't have to find baby sitters.

IDEAS FOR EMPLOYERS

- Have a flexible time-off policy. For example, employees who celebrate Jewish holidays might prefer to take off Yom Kippur and work on Christmas Day.
- Be sensitive to employees' needs to spend time with their families. Limit travel demands and work commitments that pop up outside regular business hours.
- Invite children to perform at a company party. Schedule a children's choir, a children's theater group, or individual children who like to sing or play a musical instrument.
- Find out what school and congregational activities are on your employees' schedules. Avoid scheduling work meetings at those times.
- Show your interest. Ask employees about the activities and clubs their children enjoy. Make a bulletin board of newspaper clippings and photos about children's teams and clubs.

IDEAS FOR LIBRARIANS

- Have a book-making workshop where a child can write a book and have it bound. Or plan a paper-making demonstration.
- Designate an annual or monthly "Read Together Day" to encourage families to read together at home. Distribute a list of recommended books that families can share.
- Create displays of children's books that highlight the constructive use of time assets. For example, make a display about a variety of artists or artistic styles to promote Asset 17: Creative Activities.
- Have a poster and slogan contest for children as part of Reading Is Fun week (the third week of April). Post children's entries around the library. Invite the public to cast ballots to select winners in several age categories.

IDEAS FOR COMMUNITY LEADERS

- Identify weak areas in programs and services for children. For example, do programs meet the needs of children with disabilities? Are programs and services inexpensive? Are scholarships available? What about programs for children whose first language isn't English? Plan ways to fill the gaps. Bring together leaders from schools, community organizations, recreation departments, and congregations to discuss your community's plan for children's activities.

- Set up a children's art exhibit in your city or town hall. Have an unveiling event and serve milk and cookies.

- Create a community directory or calendar listing the creative activities offered in your community. Include the names of private music instructors, too. Make the directory or calendar available at local stores and schools, or mail copies to homes.

- Help start an interfaith network in your community (if one isn't in place already). Talk with clergy members about developing asset-building strategies and programs.

- Do students ride public transportation to school? If so, talk to the community transportation board about expanding the program so older children can have rides to and from extracurricular activities.

We encourage you to photocopy this page (set the image size at 125 percent), cut out the "Ideas for Children," and share them with a child you know.

IDEAS FOR CHILDREN:
BUILDING YOUR OWN
CONSTRUCTIVE USE OF TIME ASSETS

- Make music a part of your life. Listen to it. Play it. Sing it. Dance to it.

- What are some things you like to do? Do you like to sing? play basketball? draw? Join clubs or groups where you can do these things, or do them on your own.

- Go to religious services with your family. Talk about your beliefs.

- Do arts and crafts that use your imagination. For example, if you like animals, make doggie treats or catnip toys. Or start drawing and see what your imagination creates.

- Pretend you're a movie director. Create an interesting story. Act it out with your family and friends, or make a video.

- Do something fun with your family. Put together a puzzle, bake cookies, build a model, or do a craft project together. Have a family game of throw and catch.

THE COMMITMENT
TO LEARNING ASSETS

Infants are born curious and ready to learn. To keep this excitement and involvement growing, adults need to understand children's development and choose fun and appropriate activities for them. When something catches a child's attention, caring adults can nurture that interest and find ways to help the child learn more. While it's important to keep all children engaged in learning, it's essential to build a strong foundation for learning in infants and toddlers.

The commitment to learning category includes five developmental assets for children from birth through age 11:

The Commitment to Learning Assets

Asset 21: Achievement Expectation and Motivation

Asset 22: Children Are Engaged in Learning

Asset 23: Stimulating Activity and Homework

Asset 24: Enjoyment of Learning and Bonding to School

Asset 25: Reading for Pleasure

When Search Institute surveyed 6th graders, they found that some children experience some of the commitment to learning assets more than others. Here are the percentages of these children who reported each of the assets in their lives:*

Asset 21: Achievement Motivation   **70%**

Asset 22: School Engagement   **66%**

Asset 23: Homework   **43%**

Asset 24: Bonding to School   **64%**

Asset 25: Reading for Pleasure   **33%**

---

*Some of the asset names in the survey of 6th graders are different from those relating to younger children. The survey's asset names are the names that apply to older children and teens. The asset names in *What Young Children Need to Succeed* take into account developmental and situational differences of young children. See pages 3–5 for further information about asset language.

Asset 21

ACHIEVEMENT EXPECTATION AND MOTIVATION

**Family members are motivated to do well
at work, school, and in the community, providing
a model for children. As children grow, they want
to do well in school and other activities.**

How Search Institute defines this asset . . .

For infants and toddlers: Family members are motivated to do well at work, at school, and in the community, and model their motivation for children.

For preschoolers: Parents and other adults convey and reinforce expectations to do well at work, at school, in the community, and within the family.

For elementary-age children: Children are motivated to do well in school and other activities.

ALL CHILDREN

- Children need to know and observe motivated, successful adults. Do all that you can to help children spend time with adults who want to succeed at work, at home, and in volunteer activities.
- Let children play with toys *they* like. This helps them find their motivation *inside*—they're having fun to please themselves, not to please others.

- Motivation lasts longer when it comes from within. Instead of pressuring children to do something, let them follow their interests and do what they enjoy.
- Break difficult tasks into small, manageable pieces to help children feel successful more often. A big task can be overwhelming and discouraging.
- Help children find answers and learn more about things that interest them. When a child asks you a question, give her an answer. If you aren't sure what she wants to know, say, "I'm not sure what you mean. Could you tell me more?"

INFANTS

- Show how pleased you are when infants master new skills. For example, say, "Look at that! You can hold your head up all by yourself!" Expect infants to grow and develop.
- Provide age-appropriate toys for infants. Show them different ways to play with these toys: they can shake, roll, bang, rub, and slide them. Demonstrate special things a toy can do (for example, show how to make a musical stuffed animal play a song). Give infants plenty of time to experiment and enjoy their toys on their own.

 DID YOU KNOW?

In a landmark study, researchers found that the children who have a positive and stable relationship with a parent are better able to achieve. Infants show this through an eagerness to learn more about the world around them. If they feel a secure connection to their mothers, they're more likely to feel safe to leave their mother's side and explore.

Source: L. Matas, R.A. Arend, and L.A. Sroufe, "Continuity of Adaptation in the Second Year: The Relationship Between Quality of Attachment and Later Competence." *Child Development* 49 (1978).

- Help parents and infants spend time together and form strong attachments. These attachments help babies feel safe to explore. One way to offer support is by spending an hour or two with a family's other children, giving parents some time alone with their baby.

TODDLERS

- Find ways for toddlers to develop new skills while they play with toys. For example, you might ask a toddler, "Can you put all the blue toys in a pile?" or "Can you line up all the toys with wheels?"
- Give toddlers a chance to figure things out for themselves, but step in and help them if they get frustrated.
- Praise toddlers when they proudly show you what they made. A toddler may say, "Look what I did!" Respond with, "Yes, you did! You're getting to be so big!"
- Watch toddlers when they say, "Look at me!" Talk about what you see them doing. What you say and how you say it lets them know that they can do challenging things.
- Turn off the television and the computer and give toddlers interesting toys, books, and art supplies. This gives toddlers a chance to explore, experiment, and play.

PRESCHOOLERS

- Ask preschoolers questions to help them develop their thinking skills. When a preschooler asks *you* a question, do your best to give a simple answer. Too much information can overwhelm a child. If you don't know the answer, take a trip to the library together to find out more.
- Use rewards and incentives sparingly with preschoolers. Children who need a reward to get them to do something can have trouble motivating themselves later. When children are young, your pleasure in their accomplishments is a great motivator. When they're older, they'll learn to be proud of themselves.
- Preschoolers learn a lot through play. Activity and learning are closely linked during the preschool years when children's bodies, minds, and nervous systems are growing rapidly.

- Give preschoolers time to play with puzzles, clay, board games, building block sets, and other toys that require picking up and handling small things. This will improve their eye-and-hand coordination, making it easier for them to learn to hold a pencil and write when they start school.

- Let preschoolers occasionally do things *their* way instead of *your* way. Say, "There are lots of ways to do most things. Can you think of some other ways we might do this?" Give one of their ideas a try.

RESOURCE

The Parents' and Teachers' Guide to Helping Young Children Learn, edited by Betty Farber, M.Ed. (Cutchogue, NY: Preschool Publications, 1997), gives practical ways to motivate young children to learn, using ideas from 35 respected experts in the field.

ELEMENTARY-AGE CHILDREN

- Keep an eye on children's study habits. Some children rush through their schoolwork, practice, or lessons and don't develop the skills they need. Others dawdle and procrastinate, which also keeps them from learning. Expect this to happen now and then, but intervene if it becomes a regular problem.

- Ask children "What if?" questions to help them look at the world in a different way. Your questions could be silly or serious. For example, you might say, "What if we wore roller skates instead of shoes every day?" or "What if we didn't have stop signs?" Questions like this help children think creatively.

- When children are frustrated, resist the urge to take over and make everything better. Listen to a child's feelings. Ask questions to help her work through the problem.

- Help children develop a sense of control over their lives, which will make them more motivated. They're more interested in learning when they feel like they're in charge.

- Teach children to "stick with it." Each day, work with them on their reading or math skills and show them how helpful practice can be. (This also builds Asset 23: Stimulating Activity and Homework and Asset 25: Reading for Pleasure.) Tell them about—or better yet, *show* them—something you've had to practice to learn.

- Use spontaneous rewards with no strings attached. If you expect children to work hard and learn new skills, they probably will. Instead of saying "I'll take you to the park if you finish your assignment," say, "You finished your assignment? Great! Let's go to the park to celebrate."

ASSETS IN ACTION
Motivating Children to Succeed

Kent Gulden, D.D.S., builds assets by sponsoring a Bikes for Books contest three times a year for children ages 6 to 13. For the past three years, the orthodontist in White Bear Lake, Minnesota, has encouraged reading by holding contests at his practice, an elementary school, a church, and the community library. To participate, children read books, then write down the title, author, and a 25-word description for each book. At the end of the contest, Dr. Gulden puts the names of all the participants into a box. Children then pull out three names, and each winning child gets a $300 gift certificate to a local recreational equipment retailer. The winner can choose a bicycle, skis, or another outdoor-fun starter. All the children learn about the next contest and keep reading, hoping to win next time.

Dr. Gulden also displays artwork by 4th graders from a nearby elementary school. The young people's artwork covers the lobby and many office walls. On one of his office walls, the orthodontist posts all the letters and pictures that children send him.

Asset 22

CHILDREN ARE ENGAGED IN LEARNING

Parents and other adults are responsive, attentive, and involved in learning new things, sparking children's interest in learning. As children mature, they are engaged in learning.

How Search Institute defines this asset . . .

For infants, toddlers, and preschoolers: Parents and family members model responsive and attentive attitudes at work, at school, in the community, and at home.

For elementary-age children: Children are responsive, attentive, and actively engaged in learning.

ALL CHILDREN

- Introduce children to adults who have different jobs, hobbies, traditions, and beliefs. Ask these adults to talk about their experiences with children.
- Talk with children many times throughout the day—during meals, at bathtime, and before bed. Give them your full attention. Use new words and make language fun.
- Let children follow their own interests. Give them help, but let them move forward on their own as their interest grows.

- Develop your own interests so children see that you enjoy learning, too. For example, if you always wanted to play the trombone, rent or buy the instrument and take lessons, teach yourself with books, or get pointers from a neighbor who used to play.

RESOURCE

The Growth of the Mind by Stanley I. Greenspan (Reading, MA: Addison Wesley, 1997) stresses that intelligence is more than being smart—a child's emotions and an interest in learning are important, too.

INFANTS

- Meet the infant's needs. Pay attention to cues that the infant is trying to tell you something. For example, an infant who cries and tugs at his ear may have an ear infection. An infant who drools and chews on things may have teething pain. Infants who are surrounded by adults who respond to them are more likely to grow up to be confident in and comfortable with themselves.
- Give infants plenty of time to investigate the things that interest them. For example, if an infant laughs and gurgles when she sees herself in a mirror, let her keep looking until she gets bored. (She'll let you know this by looking away or squirming.)
- Play with infants. Babies often enjoy their toys more when someone plays along with them.
- Let infants grow and develop at their own pace. For example, it's normal for a baby to start walking at 9 months and also normal at 18 months. If you're worried that an infant is developing too slowly, talk to a medical professional about your concerns.
- Shake a rattle, then give it to an infant to play with. Infants like to try things they've seen other people do. When an infant is interested in a toy, give him plenty of time to experiment with it instead of interrupting him with something new.

- When crawlers take off for a specific toy, don't immediately interrupt their attention with a different one. Wait until they no longer seem interested before introducing a new toy.

TODDLERS

- Find ways to build on a toddler's enthusiasm and share her excitement. For example, if a toddler squeals with joy when she sees a dump truck, take her to a construction site to watch more equipment at work. Visit the library together and check out picture books about machines. Give her a toy truck to play with.

- Let toddlers explore the natural world. Help them learn more about things that interest them. For example, some toddlers are fascinated by the "busyness" of ants. If so, help them build an ant farm. With the help of an adult, children can watch the ants through a magnifying glass and learn more about what the ants are doing. Show your excitement about the things they enjoy. Your reaction can engage them even further.

- Toddlers often like to hear the same books over and over again. (This also builds Asset 25: Reading for Pleasure.) Stay enthusiastic and let toddlers get tired of an activity before you do. Hearing the same story many times in a row helps them build language skills.

- Talk with toddlers during mealtimes, bathtimes, and changing times. Give them your full attention. Use new words and make language fun.

PRESCHOOLERS

- Make sure preschoolers have enough to eat and plenty of rest. Hungry, tired preschoolers will have trouble learning and paying attention.

- Some children are curious and ask questions when adults are around. Other children like to explore on their own. Create an atmosphere for learning that fits each child's personality.

- Use music, puzzles, books, blocks, dramatic play, and games to add variety and interest to a preschooler's day. Give preschoolers new activities to enjoy. These activities will broaden their interests and keep them engaged in learning through play.

- Play the "Why?" game. With a preschooler, take turns asking and answering "Why?" questions. If you're stumped, find the answer together.

- Talk to preschoolers about their feelings. Let them know that feelings aren't right or wrong—they just are. Help them use their problem-solving skills to find ways to handle their feelings. For example, if a child is sad, you might say, "I feel sad sometimes, too. Let's talk about it."

ELEMENTARY-AGE CHILDREN

- Don't expect all of children's learning to happen in school. Keep stretching children's minds with stories, games, and activities whenever you're together. Find ways for children to learn more about a topic that interests them. For example, if a child is fascinated by space, check out books about space from the library, search out information on the Internet, or visit an air and space museum together. Help the child write a letter to an astronaut. Learn more about space separately and together.

- When you talk about a child's school, stay positive. Let the child know that you think school is fun and important.

- When children are bored and look for things to do, have them come up with their own solutions. Make sure there are plenty of interesting books, games, and other materials to spark their interest.

- Engage children's imagination. When they're struggling with an issue, have children pretend they're someone else. For example, if a child feels left out of a play group, ask the child what Henry (from the "Boxcar" series by Gertrude Chandler Warner) or Ramona (a Beverly Cleary character) would do.

Asset 23

STIMULATING ACTIVITY AND HOMEWORK

Parents, caregivers, and teachers are mindful of children's individual needs as they provide opportunities for play, learning, and exploration. Elementary-age children do homework when it's assigned.

How Search Institute defines this asset . . .

For infants, toddlers, and preschoolers: Parents encourage children to explore and provide stimulating toys that match children's emerging skills. Parents are sensitive to children's dispositions, preferences, and level of development.

For elementary-age children: Parents and teachers encourage children to explore and engage in stimulating activities. Children do homework when it's assigned.

ALL CHILDREN

- Take children to visit parks, malls, aquariums, museums, and sculpture gardens so they can see lots of different, interesting things.
- Be available when children have questions, but don't be an "answer person." Ask more questions to get children thinking or guide them to resources that will help them learn more.

- Make music part of children's environment. Sing to them or play recorded music whenever you can. (Children's book and toy stores often have a good selection of recordings for kids. You can also borrow tapes and CDs from the library.)

INFANTS

- Show newborns high-contrast or black-and-white pictures. Add pictures with more colors and details as infants grow older.
- Find ways for older infants to use their sense of touch. Let them pat and squeeze soft stuffed animals, hard blocks, smooth yogurt, and lumpy oatmeal.
- Use rattles and other noisemakers to make many interesting sounds for infants to hear.
- Hold an infant while you're in front of a large mirror. Go up close to the mirror and let the infant take a closer look. Make funny faces and see what the infant does.
- Young children use their mouths to explore the world and learn. Expect babies (and toddlers) to put lots of things in their mouths. Give children teething rings, pacifiers, and other child-safe toys.

RESOURCE

Games Babies Play collected by Vicki Lansky (Minnetonka, MN: Book Peddlers, 1993) is filled with fun playtime activities for children ages birth to 12 months.

TODDLERS

- Spend time outdoors with toddlers. Look at grass and leaves together and watch cars and people go by. Ask toddlers to describe what they see. For example, you might say, "Tell me about the tree by the side of the road."
- Play "Name that Sound." Either mimic different sounds (like a truck, bird, or siren) or when you hear sounds (such as an airplane passing overhead or a dog barking in the distance), ask toddlers what they hear.

- Give toddlers different things to touch—finger paints, a piece of sandpaper, a feather, a rubber snake, a ball, or stickers with the back taken off. Name the sensations for toddlers (such as rough, smooth, sticky, and so on). Ask toddlers what they think about these things. For example, a toddler might say, "I don't like this one," or "That one tickles me."
- As they get more teeth, toddlers will put more things in their mouth. Many toddlers will chew on whatever is nearby, so keep dangerous items out of reach. Sometimes a warm, damp washcloth will interest them and soothe the mouth pain that comes with teething.

Preschoolers

- Teach preschoolers fun games like "Simon Says" and "Red Light, Green Light" to help them learn to play with others, follow instructions, and have fun at the same time.
- Do creative crafts together. Make handprints or footprints with finger paints on large sheets of parcel paper. Have children glue dried leaves and flowers to construction paper to make nature collages.

RESOURCE

Wonderplay by Fretta Reitzes and Beth Teitelman with Lois Alter Mark (Philadelphia: Running Press, 1995) contains more than 200 interactive and developmental games, crafts, and creative activities for infants, toddlers, and preschoolers. The ideas in this book were created at the Parenting Center at the 92nd Street Y, New York City's world-renowned community and cultural center.

- Hold a smelling extravaganza. Blindfold preschoolers and tell them to rate each smell as "yummy" or "yucky." Let them smell perfume, herbs, spices, vinegar, flowers, and a smelly sock.
- Play "Follow the Leader." Have preschoolers do challenging motions, like hopping on one foot, walking backward, skipping, and sitting down and then standing up.

- Make up memory and naming games. For example, tape a coin to a piece of plain cardboard and turn it over so children can't see the coin. Make two cards for each type of coin. Have preschoolers turn over two cards at a time to see which coins they get. Have them "hide" the coins again and turn over two more until they get a match.

- Find unusual foods for preschoolers to sample. Ask them about their favorite flavors and smells.

ELEMENTARY-AGE CHILDREN

- Set up a special place for children to do homework. This could be at a table in a quiet corner of the living room, a desk in the child's bedroom, or another area in the home that's not too busy or noisy. Make sure children have plenty of pencils, paper, and any other supplies they need.

- Help children plan and chart long-term assignments (which also builds Asset 32: Planning and Decision Making). Teach children how to work slowly and complete a little at a time instead of cramming everything in at the last minute.

- Help children make homework a part of their evening routine. Keep the learning habit going by having fun backup projects ready when a child doesn't have homework.

- Children often have 10 minutes of homework per grade level. For example, 1st graders may have 10 minutes of homework at night, while 5th graders might have 50 minutes.

- Be directly involved with younger children (ages 6 through 8) as they do homework. Give them plenty of help and advice, but remember that their homework is *theirs*, not yours. As children get older, they can work more independently. By the time they're 10 or 11, they should be able to do most of their homework on their own. Check to see that they've finished their assignments and give them help when they need it.

- Set an example for learning. While children do homework, sit quietly nearby and take a few minutes to read a book or practice a skill.

DID YOU KNOW?

Here are three key ways to teach a child to take responsibility for his homework:

- Help the child set up a special homework area.
- Develop a homework routine with the child.
- Help the child when he needs assistance with a homework assignment.

Source: Lynn Corno, "Homework Is a Compliance Thing." *Educational Researcher* 25, no. 8 (1996).

- Are you an expert in a subject? If so, offer to help children in a neighborhood school with homework in that area.

RESOURCES

Homework Improvement by Roberta Schneiderman (Glenview, IL: Good Year Books, 1996) is a parent's guide to helping children develop lifelong, successful homework habits.

How to Help Your Child with Homework by Marguerite C. Radencich, Ph.D., and Jeanne Shay Schumm, Ph.D. (Minneapolis: Free Spirit Publishing, 1997), is filled with advice from teachers on how to halt homework battles and help children with reading, math, science, test preparation, and more.

Asset 24

ENJOYMENT OF LEARNING AND BONDING TO SCHOOL

Parents and other adults model their enjoyment of learning and find engaging learning activities for children. Elementary-age children care about their school.

How Search Institute defines this asset . . .

For infants: Parents enjoy learning and model this through their own learning activities.

For toddlers: Parents enjoy learning and express this through their own learning activities.

For preschoolers: Parents and other adults enjoy learning and engage preschoolers in learning activities.

For elementary-age children: Children enjoy learning and care about their school.

ALL CHILDREN

- Make "look-at-this" moments part of your everyday life. Be enthusiastic about things you discover (such as a bird's nest in a tree) and show them to children.

- On trips and excursions, point out details children may not have noticed before. At the zoo, you might say, "Look at all the colors in the peacock's tail! How many do you see?"
- Give children creative, fun challenges. Ask, "What could we make with this empty cardboard box and this paint and paintbrush?"

INFANTS

- Use routine events as an opportunity for learning. For example, at changing time, clap the infant's hands and move his legs around. Count his fingers and toes.
- Talk, talk, talk to infants. To learn language, children need to hear real words. Don't use "baby talk," but do keep your tone lively and use an "up" inflection.
- When you smile, make happy faces, or stick out your tongue, an infant will mimic you. Pay attention to how the infant reacts. Stop if she isn't having fun, gets bored with this game, or starts to cry.
- Exaggerate some of the day-to-day activities you do with an infant. For example, gently rock a baby in your arms very slowly or to a musical beat. Do this for as long as the infant enjoys it.

TODDLERS

- Be patient with toddlers when they're learning new things. Remember that accidents happen. For example, stay calm when a toddler tips over his juice. You might say, "Uh, oh! We have a river. Can you help me wipe up the river before it becomes a waterfall and splashes over the edge of the table?"
- Looking for a fun and inexpensive toy for a toddler? Try a Ping-Pong ball. Toddlers love making Ping-Pong balls bounce all over the room.
- Sing when you do simple chores. Choose songs that toddlers know so they can sing along with you. For example, toddlers might like to sing the alphabet song while helping pick up toys. Teach them new songs, too, with simple hand motions.

RESOURCE

USA Toy Library Association
2530 Crawford Avenue, Suite 111
Evanston, IL 60201
Telephone: (847) 864-3330
Web site: *www.sjdccd.cc.ca.us/toylibrary*

While older children show how much they enjoy learning by caring about their school, young children begin to enjoy learning through play. This organization helps develop toy lending libraries and other programs that help young children have fun as they learn.

- Make silly faces at toddlers you know. Smile when they make a funny face back at you.
- Ooh and ahh when toddlers tell you wild, imaginative stories. Ask questions to keep the stories going.

Preschoolers

- Play "Can you do this?" with preschoolers. Jump up and down and ask toddlers if they can do what you just did. Try other motions, such as sitting down and moving your feet in the air, or clapping your hands.
- Keep a box of dress-up clothes (including accessories and shoes) handy to spark preschoolers' imaginations. Dressing up is fun for girls *and* boys.
- Have preschoolers help you in the kitchen. Together, make cookies, cake, macaroni and cheese, and other simple foods they like. They can mix and measure the ingredients while you use the stove, oven, microwave, or other appliances. Be patient with messes.
- Use things from the preschooler's world to teach numbers and the alphabet. For example, ask preschoolers to count the number of carrot sticks they have as they eat a snack.
- Ask preschoolers questions about their favorite subjects. For example, some preschoolers know the names of many dinosaurs or endangered animals. Some know the names of many pieces

of farm equipment. By asking questions, you show you're interested in what they know.

ELEMENTARY-AGE CHILDREN

- Children who feel a bond to their school have connections with their teachers. Ask teachers (including the classroom, music, physical education, and art teachers, as well as other specialists) to share something about themselves with their students.

 DID YOU KNOW?

There's more to school than learning skills. It's equally important that children form a bond to school, which helps them learn to accept the goals of learning and behave in appropriate ways. Researchers show that when children like their school, they're more likely to be successful and achieve academically.

Source: K. McNamara, "Bonding to School and the Development of Responsibility." *Journal of Emotional and Behavioral Problems* 4 (1996).

- If you're able, purchase school T-shirts, caps, sweatshirts, or other clothing that's for sale. Wearing these things helps children show their pride in their school.
- Play "Stump the experts." Research an interesting topic with a child, then have other people ask the two of you questions about what you learn.
- Help children make friends with their schoolmates. Let a child invite a special friend over for dinner, for a sleepover, or just to hang around.
- Learn what children like most about school. Ask specific questions about music, gym, art, recess, and lunch. (Don't be alarmed if children like lunch or recess best. What's important is that they're excited about something at school.)
- Make informal learning experiences fun and exciting to teach children that learning is important—and interesting—outside

of school, too. Compare prices at the grocery store. Read billboards and street signs. Outdoors, observe and study nature.

 ## ASSETS IN ACTION
Nurturing a Commitment to Learning

One elementary school principal doesn't wait until children enter kindergarten to begin building assets—she begins the day they're born. For the past seven years, Wanda Schlesser, the principal of West Elementary, has been sending a letter to each baby born in New Richmond, Wisconsin. Ms. Schlesser hopes this can help her establish a relationship with the child and the parents. "Kids who aren't old enough to come to my school start to get to know me when I write to them," she says. In the letter, she writes about how her elementary school already has a desk for the child. For the parents, she includes information about raising a child, along with asset-building materials. Then she sends a different letter on the child's first, second, third, and fourth birthdays—until the child comes through the school doors as a kindergartner. She keeps track of 700 to 800 children this way. It takes a lot of time, but she feels it's worth it. "Education doesn't start when a child is five years old," Ms. Schlesser says. "It starts at birth, and maybe even sooner."

Asset 25

READING
FOR PLEASURE

Parents and other adults read to all children, make reading fun, and encourage participation. Preschool and elementary-age children read with adults at least 30 minutes each day and also enjoy reading on their own.

How Search Institute defines this asset . . .

For infants: Parents read to infants in enjoyable ways every day.

For toddlers: Parents read to toddlers every day and find ways for toddlers to participate in enjoyable reading experiences.

For preschoolers: Adults read to preschoolers for at least 30 minutes over the course of a day, encouraging preschoolers to participate.

For elementary-age children: Children and an adult read together for at least 30 minutes a day. Children also enjoy reading or looking at books or magazines on their own.

ALL CHILDREN

- Take children to the library or bookstore regularly. Help them choose books to look at or read together. Give books as a gift and explain that buying and reading books is a good way to spend time and money.

RESOURCE

Reading Is Fundamental (RIF)
600 Maryland Avenue SW, Suite 600
Washington, DC 20024-2520
Telephone: (202) 287-3220
Toll-free phone: 1-877-RIF-READ (1-877-743-7323)
Web site: *www.rif.org*
This organization sponsors programs that get young children ready for reading and inspire older children to read. As of the year 2000, RIF will have put 200 million books into the hands and homes of America's children. Contact the organization to ask for materials and find out more.

- Parents' enthusiasm for books is contagious. Be a reader yourself!
- Read all kinds of books and magazines together. Choose reading material that introduces children to new experiences, ideas, and cultures.

INFANTS

- Start reading to infants as soon as they're born. Read aloud parts of the daily newspaper, a magazine, a novel, poems, or children's stories. It doesn't matter what you read—for infants, the sound of your voice and the quiet time you share is most important.
- Make books a part of everyday life for infants. Give them board books and touch-and-feel books like *Pat the Bunny* by Dorothy Kunhardt (New York: Golden Books, 1990). Infants especially like books with simple rhymes or pictures of animals or baby faces.
- Snuggle with infants as you look at books together. This helps make reading pleasurable.

DID YOU KNOW?

Reading to children, even infants, can help them in a number of ways. For example, one study of 2-year-olds and their mothers focused on the age of children when their mothers began reading to them, how often this happened, the number of stories they read, and how often the child visited a local library. The researchers saw that children who had picture books read to them were able to understand what was being said sooner than other children. In addition, those children whose mothers began reading to them when the children were infants started talking and using language before other children did.

Source: B.D. DeBaryshe, "Joint Picture-Book Reading Correlates of Early Oral Language Skill." *Journal of Child Language* 20 (1993).

TODDLERS

- When you're sharing a book with young toddlers, look at the pictures together before you read the words. Have the toddlers talk about what they see to help them build language skills. As toddlers grow older and are learning how to listen, start reading parts of the story.

- Let a toddler turn the pages. Expect him to skip pages or want to look at books upside down or backward. Don't worry about reading the "right" way—just let him have fun with the book.

- Read books every day. Toddlers may wander away now and then, but they usually will wander back. Be patient as they learn to sit and listen while you read aloud.

- Cuddle and snuggle with a toddler when you read to her.

- Fill a basket or bucket full of books for toddlers. When it's reading time, ask them to pick two or three books they'd like to share.

PRESCHOOLERS

- Let preschoolers' reading skills develop at their own pace. Don't push them to start reading before they're ready. Teach them the basics in fun ways. For example, say, "Can you tell me what letter is on the sign over there?"
- Play a rhyme game with preschoolers. Start simple rhymes and have preschoolers finish them for you. For example, say, "Way up in the sky, the little birds. . . ."
- Find picture books that don't have any words on the page, such as *Time Flies* by Eric Rohmann (New York: Crown Books, 1994). Ask preschoolers to tell you a story to match the pictures.
- Go on a reading hunt and look for things with words on them. At a grocery store, preschoolers will find words on magazines and newspapers, food packages, advertisements, money, shopping lists, and more.
- Books make great gifts for a preschooler. Help her build her personal library and explain that books truly *are* gifts. Say, "I love getting books as presents! Books take us on great adventures."

ELEMENTARY-AGE CHILDREN

- Keep reading aloud to children, even when they're able to read by themselves. Reading together helps strengthen your relationship with the child. Have children read aloud to you, too.
- Find books that get children excited about reading. Some children like fiction. Some children like biographies of sports heroes. Still others might like comic books. Let children read what they like.
- Reading is for everyone! Sometimes children think reading is "dorky." Let them know that it's cool to read.
- A child's interest in reading will ebb and flow. During the slow times, suggest books about a topic that interests the child to get him reading again.
- Challenge children to use the newspaper to answer questions. You might ask, "Which basketball player has scored the most points this season?" or "What animal was just taken off the endangered species list?"

ASSETS IN ACTION
Making Reading Exciting

Third-grade teacher Janet Muller, her 25 students at Duniway Elementary School in Portland, Oregon, and their parents get together once a month at the Dragon's Breath Cafe to read and discuss a children's book. Ms. Muller believes that fun activities like this—plus cookies and hot chocolate—bring families closer, giving them a sense of connectedness and a shared love of reading.

MORE IDEAS FOR BUILDING THE COMMITMENT TO LEARNING ASSETS

IDEAS FOR PARENTS

- Model your commitment to learning. If you want to learn how to do woodworking, for example, take a class and start doing small projects at home.

- Stay on top of happenings at your child's school. Read newsletters and other information that your children bring home. Ask questions about what you read. Your interest will help children bond with their school.

- Find out what your children are learning in school. Come up with ways for them to learn more about the areas they enjoy. Focus on children's accomplishments and attitudes instead of just their grades.

- Set aside time for supervised learning in your family schedule. Older children can work on their homework while younger children enjoy fun learning activities.

- Take family trips to interesting places. Visit a cave at a state park or a touring exhibit at a museum. Contact your city or state department of tourism and ask for free brochures and information on places you might like.

- Have regular family reading times. Curl up together as one person reads a book out loud. If all your children can read on their own, you might choose to hang out together and read your own books.

IDEAS FOR CHILDCARE PROVIDERS

- Create an environment that promotes learning and creativity. Build on children's skills and imagination by doing new projects and activities as part of a predictable, consistent routine.
- Share books with the children in your care. Set aside time each day for reading. Check out books from a local library or visit used bookstores for bargains.

 ASSETS IN ACTION
A Teaching Childcare Center

Orchard Valley Learning Center in Aurora, Colorado, was one of the first childcare centers in the country to include asset building as part of its program. All staff members learn about the 40 developmental assets, and the 40-week curriculum cycle covers each of the assets in turn. At a series of parent workshops, the center provides asset-building training for parents, too. "There's a genuine concern for kids here," says Jacque Montgomery, the mother of two children who attend the center. Here are some of Orchard Valley's asset-building efforts:

- Children practice using words and negotiating skills instead of fighting (Asset 36: Peaceful Conflict Resolution).
- High school students read books to toddlers (Asset 25: Reading for Pleasure).
- Senior citizens rock babies in the infant room (Asset 3: Other Adult Relationships).
- Three-year-olds vote about what game to play during outdoor time (Asset 7: Community Values Children and Asset 32: Planning and Decision Making).
- The center has a service project (Asset 8: Children Are Given Useful Roles and Asset 9: Service to Others) called a "warm fuzzy drive" where families collect hats, scarves, and mittens to donate to children at a local school.

- Build a library for each childcare room. Ask parents, caregivers, and members of the community to donate appropriate books.
- Give children a chance to immerse themselves in a toy or activity. Notice children's interest and concentration. You might say, "You really like that puzzle, don't you?" Spend some time with the child doing what he likes to do.
- Hire staff members who are curious and want to try new things. These attitudes rub off on children.

IDEAS FOR EDUCATORS

- Find creative ways to make learning fun. Have students make up rhymes about science facts or short plays about events in history.
- Help children show their school pride. Teach them their school song or the song of a local high school—or have them compose a song of their own. Do art projects that use the school colors.
- Have children plan and prepare for school parties. Make place mats and name tags. Research the history of the event or holiday you're celebrating.
- Have a classroom reading challenge. At the beginning of the school year, create a 6-foot-tall bookmark and hang it on the wall. As you read books to the class (and as children read books themselves), keep a tally and fill in part of the bookmark. Let children who aren't reading on their own mark the books that their parents read to them. At the end of the school year, make a big deal out of the total number of books the class has read.
- Give children meaningful homework assignments each day—not busywork. Plan extra challenges for children who finish all their work. For example, children could interview parents, siblings, grandparents, aunts, and uncles about their favorite building in the world and why they like it.
- Keep track of what captures children's attention and enthusiasm and what makes their eyes glaze over. Adjust your teaching style and methods to keep children interested. If you need help, get advice from another teacher.

- Have a program where preschoolers sing, dance, talk, or act. Invite parents and other family members. Programs like this help preschoolers and their parents form a deeper connection with the childcare setting.

IDEAS FOR HEALTH-CARE PROFESSIONALS

- Let parents know that children who eat well and get plenty of sleep are more alert and ready to learn.
- Make your waiting and examination rooms a place where children can learn. Provide plenty of books and toys for children to enjoy.
- Find out what's happening in the local school districts. Talking about these events with children you meet shows you care about what's going on at school.
- Teach parents about the power of developmental assets. Talk about how assets help make children strong, healthy, and ready to learn.
- Sponsor a clinic read-a-thon and give awards to every child who participates. Have a group photo of your readers and try to get an article about your event published in the local newspaper.

IDEAS FOR CONGREGATIONAL LEADERS

- Link children and adults who share school interests. For example, at congregational mixers, divide people into groups according to their favorite subject (math, history, science, and so on).
- Write about children in your congregational newsletter and bulletin, particularly when they take part in a school fair or school event. Each fall, make a list of the names, grade levels, and schools of the children in your congregation. Include this list in a newsletter or bulletin.
- Make a congregational library of books that fit your religious beliefs. Include books for children as well as adults.
- Are your congregation's religious education materials age-appropriate and interesting? If not, change or adapt the curriculum, or create your own.

- Set up an after-school homework help program once a week (or more often, if you can). Arrange for adult volunteers to be tutors. If possible, provide transportation for children who attend. Plan some fun activities for children to do when they finish their homework.

- Donate materials that schools can use. For example, a congregation could create school-supply kits for children who can't afford them, or raise money to help a nearby school expand its playground.

IDEAS FOR EMPLOYERS

- Make it easy for employees to volunteer as readers, tutors, or homework helpers. Post lists of volunteer opportunities that are available at nearby schools.

- Create a company climate that promotes learning. As part of your company's benefit package, consider paying tuition fees for employees who continue their education.

- Contribute money, time, or resources to schools. Find out what kinds of things the schools could use, and make donations when possible.

- Expect employees to be responsive, attentive, and actively involved in their work. When they're not, talk with them about what you're observing right away. Emphasize that their work habits can teach children about learning habits. For example, employees who are excited about their work talk about their enthusiasm at home. This modeling shows children the importance of being engaged in what they do, whether it's working at a job, building a block tower, or learning a subject.

- Let employees show school spirit in their work areas by hanging up school banners and calendars. Decorate an employee's space with the school's colors to mark the first day of school for his kindergartner.

IDEAS FOR LIBRARIANS

- Start a children's reading group in your library. Help children identify their favorite authors and illustrators. Read these people's books together, then read their biographies or visit their Web sites to learn more about their lives. Have children write stories or draw pictures inspired by their work. Encourage children to write letters to their favorite authors and illustrators and ask them questions. (Get in touch with the person's publisher to find out where to send the letters.)
- Display books that children have created and written in school or on their own.
- Offer a reading program to encourage children to read a certain number of books over a school break. When they've reached their goal, give them a free book, a button, and a certificate.
- Create a mobile library to visit children who don't have access to your building. If you already have a mobile program, find out what you can do to make it more effective.
- Set up a program to celebrate people in your community—children and adults—who learn to read. An adult who's learning how to read might inspire a 1st grader who's struggling with reading.

IDEAS FOR COMMUNITY LEADERS

- Create community events that children will enjoy. For example, have the fire department, the police department, the local hospital, the city bus company, and a funeral home set up their vehicles for children to look at and ask questions about.
- Do people know about all of the museums and historical sites in your community? Create a list of these and other places families can visit to learn and have fun. If possible, publish the list in an attractive brochure and distribute it to everyone in the community.
- Encourage the school board and the community council to work together to build assets. Introduce an asset-building resolution or have the council declare an "Asset-Building Day" in your community.

- Have school board members or school administrators update your community council about important events at each school. Let community members know what's happening and when.
- Talk to school administrators and board members about the U.S. Department of Education's Blue Ribbon Schools Program, which recognizes outstanding American schools. For more information on how to apply for this honor, contact the U.S. Department of Education, 400 Maryland Avenue SW, Washington, DC 20202-0498; toll-free phone: 1-800-USA-LEARN (1-800-872-5327); Web site: *www.ed.gov/*.
- Create a handbook or calendar of information about the school district. List phone numbers, contact people, school hours, and brief descriptions of each area school.

We encourage you to photocopy this page (set the image size at 125 percent), cut out the "Ideas for Children," and share them with a child you know.

IDEAS FOR CHILDREN: BUILD YOUR OWN COMMITMENT TO LEARNING ASSETS

- Learn more about the things that interest you. Do you like bugs? Hunt for bugs you haven't seen before. Are you curious about what makes a plane fly? Find a book about it at the library or bookstore, or build a model airplane.
- Always do your best. You don't know what you can do until you try.
- Pay attention at school. Listen to your teacher, and talk to the teacher if you feel that your schoolwork is too hard or too easy.
- Ask lots of questions. Have adults help you find answers.
- Read, read, read. Then read some more. Read what you like. Reading is one of the main ways people learn new things.
- Take a reading adventure—visit the library often. Explore a new section of the library.
- Try learning about something new. Memorize a knock-knock joke. Learn a yo-yo trick. Be creative!

THE POSITIVE
VALUES ASSETS

Values are the important internal compasses that guide children to make decisions and set priorities. Children's thoughts and actions are based on their values—even if these values aren't yet fully developed. Parents and other adults can help children identify positive values and make them a part of their lives. When children have positive values, they grow into caring adults who set high standards for themselves and the people around them.

The positive values category includes six developmental assets for children from birth through age 11:

The Positive Values Assets

Asset 26: Family Values Caring

Asset 27: Family Values Equality and Social Justice

Asset 28: Family Values Integrity

Asset 29: Family Values Honesty

Asset 30: Family Values Responsibility

Asset 31: Family Values Healthy Lifestyle

When Search Institute surveyed 6th graders, they found that children experience some of the positive values assets more than others. Here are the percentages of these children who reported each of the assets in their lives:*

Asset 26: Caring	**56%**
Asset 27: Equality and Social Justice	**59%**
Asset 28: Integrity	**63%**
Asset 29: Honesty	**73%**
Asset 30: Responsibility	**65%**
Asset 31: Restraint	**71%**

*Some of the asset names in the survey of 6th graders are different from those relating to younger children. The survey's asset names are the names that apply to older children and teens. The asset names in *What Young Children Need to Succeed* take into account developmental and situational differences of young children. See pages 3–5 for further information about asset language.

Asset 26

FAMILY VALUES
CARING

All children observe parents and other adults helping people. As children mature, they learn and are encouraged to help others.

How Search Institute defines this asset . . .

For infants and toddlers: Parents convey their beliefs about helping others by modeling their helping behaviors.

For preschoolers: Preschoolers are encouraged to express sympathy for someone who is distressed and begin to develop a variety of helping behaviors.

For elementary-age children: Children are encouraged to help other people.

ALL CHILDREN

- Children watch and learn from your example. Treat other people in caring and loving ways, especially when you're around children.
- Children who feel that others care about *their* feelings are more likely to care about others themselves. Be sensitive to children's emotions and show them appropriate ways to express their feelings. Everyone feels angry or afraid once in a while. This is natural.

- Hitting and spanking hurt—and they don't teach children positive values. When children misbehave, try using helpful discipline methods such as logical consequences, redirecting, focusing on positive behavior, or time-outs instead.

RESOURCE

Teaching Your Kids to Care by Deborah Spaide (New York: Citadel Press, 1995) includes 105 creative caring activities for children in kindergarten through grade 12. It also suggests practical ways to develop a caring spirit in children.

INFANTS

- Hold infants. Smile at them. Love them. Care for them when they need you *and* when they're content.
- When an infant cries, meet his needs right away. Taking care of infants helps them feel secure and models the importance of caring for others.
- Set appropriate limits for how older infants behave. For example, when infants hurt others, say, "We don't hit people," and show them other ways to act. When they act in caring ways, let them know you approve.
- Get older siblings involved in an infant's care. Shaking a rattle, getting a diaper, or showing the baby a board book are ways a sibling can help.

TODDLERS

- Notice when toddlers act in caring ways, such as when they pat a puppy. You might say, "Thank you for being gentle with Chloé. She really likes that."
- Be positive and loving when you're with a toddler. Young children care for others in the same way they're cared for.
- Toddlers can be inconsistent in how they treat others. Sometimes they may try to console an upset playmate. At other times they may become angry themselves and hit the crying

child out of frustration. Explain to toddlers what they should—and shouldn't—do when they see an unhappy person. Emphasize that hitting doesn't show caring and is never okay.

- A toddler who sees another child crying may start crying herself. If this happens, say, "That child is feeling sad. When we see someone feeling sad, we sometimes feel sad, too." If the toddler tries to comfort the crying child, say, "It's very caring of you to try to help" or, "I can tell you care."

 DID YOU KNOW?

A classic study shows that infants and toddlers are not developmentally capable of altruism (unselfish concern for the welfare of others). However, a family's commitment to helping others lays the groundwork for instilling caring in young children. Toddlers *are* capable of sympathy, which is an early step toward altruism. Toddlers will offer a toy to a companion, help with household chores, or demonstrate compassion by trying to cheer up a distressed playmate.

Source: H.L. Rheingold, "Little Children's Participation in the Work of Adults, an Ascent Prosocial Behavior." *Child Development* 53 (1982), 114–125.

PRESCHOOLERS

- Give preschoolers simple tasks they can do to help others. Let them feed the fish one day, or bring a tool to an adult who's fixing something.
- Talk with preschoolers about positive values. Have children describe what these values mean to them. For example, you might ask, "What are some ways to show other people we care about them? Do we show we care by yelling? by talking quietly?"
- Many preschoolers have a natural urge to help others. For example, a preschooler may want to use a hug—or a cookie—to comfort a sad child. When you know how the child would like to help, try to find a way for him to do it.

- When you see people caring for each other, talk about this with preschoolers. For example, say, "Danisha must have felt scared and hurt when she fell off the swing. Her mom is there holding her and talking to her. I think that's helping Danisha feel better. What do you think?"
- Thank preschoolers who do spontaneous acts of caring and helping. You might say, "Thanks for giving that puzzle piece to Amil. That was a kind thing to do, and it helped him finish the puzzle."
- Respect preschoolers' belongings by asking before you take something (like a toy or a favorite blanket) from them. Teach respectful, caring behaviors when preschoolers take things from each other. Say, "We ask before we borrow toys."
- Take preschoolers to a hospital or another place where they can meet people who need medical care. Talk about how people are helped there. In advance, talk with preschoolers about unfamiliar things they might see, such as intravenous tubes or ventilators.

ELEMENTARY-AGE CHILDREN

- Taking care of animals is a great way to teach children about caring. Children might care for a family or classroom pet, or they could fill a birdbath with water or scatter birdseed for birds and squirrels.
- If children see someone who needs help (for example, if they witness an accident), talk with them about what they saw. A situation like this may be confusing or frightening to a child. Help children share their feelings and understand the situation.
- Do a fund-raising activity together. Participate in a bike-a-thon, walk-a-thon, or sing-a-thon. Talk about how important such acts of caring can be.
- Find ways for children to work directly with people who need care. Having children collect cans of food may be easy, but the more complicated task of serving food at a shelter will bring children face-to-face with the people they're helping. This lets them know how important their care and concern really are.

RESOURCE

Kids Care Clubs
P.O. Box 1083
New Canaan, CT 06840
Telephone: (914) 533-1101
Web site: *www.kidscare.org*

Know children who want to help others? Have them write a letter to this organization telling why. In response, Kids Care Clubs will send ideas from other children. You can also become a member of this national organization and receive newsletters of ideas.

- If children get an allowance, encourage them to give part of it to a charity or congregation. Help them get into the habit of giving.
- Many wonderful presents don't come from a store. Children can write books, draw pictures, make crafts, and create other gifts to give.

ASSETS IN ACTION
Workers Who Care

In Georgetown, Texas, children smile, wave, and go out of their way to say hello to utility workers. They know that these workers care about children, and that they can turn to these adults if they ever need help.

When the Safe Place program was first introduced, utility workers drove their specially marked bucket trucks to all the elementary schools to speak with the 4,500 children in the community. Before they could drive one of these trucks, utility workers had to pass an extensive background check and receive two hours of training in building assets. Children learned that if they needed help, they could count on the drivers of the trucks with the special logos.

These workers help children when police officers or other adults aren't around. For example, one utility worker was approached by a boy who needed help for his friend who'd been in a bike accident. The worker made sure the friend was okay, and gave both boys (along with the damaged bike) a ride to their homes in his truck.

Asset 27

FAMILY VALUES EQUALITY AND SOCIAL JUSTICE

Parents and other adults demonstrate ways to promote equality and tolerance. As children mature, they find ways to make their community a better place.

How Search Institute defines this asset . . .

For infants, toddlers, and preschoolers: Parents place a high value on promoting social equality, religious tolerance, and reducing hunger and poverty while modeling these beliefs for children.

For elementary-age children: Children begin to show interest in making the community a better place.

ALL CHILDREN

- Children learn by watching the adults around them. Let your words and actions show that you care about equality and social justice.
- Treat children equally. Sometimes people gush over happy, cute children but act more reserved with children who are fussy or who have more ordinary looks. Be friendly toward *all* children.

INFANTS

- Support programs that help families with infants. Contribute money, time, or ideas.
- Surround infants with a warm, nurturing environment. This helps children know they're valued, making them more likely to value others.
- While you're meeting the needs of infants, remember that other people in the family have needs, too. Support and nurture everyone in the family.

TODDLERS

- Do you know anyone who might enjoy spending time with a toddler? If so, give the person a call and set up a time for you and the toddler to visit. Make the time together meaningful. Sing songs. Tell stories. Arrange a time for another visit.
- When you vote, take a toddler along. Use simple language to talk with the toddler about what the candidates want to do to help people's lives. "I'm voting for this man so he can pass laws to help poor people." "I'm voting for this woman because she cares about making things fair for everyone."
- Give toddlers lightweight cans or other easy-to-carry nonperishable foods to place in a food donation box. Talk to toddlers about how important it is to share.
- When toddlers share—especially when they do this without being prompted—let them know you like what they're doing.

PRESCHOOLERS

- Use examples to teach preschoolers about social justice. In a lesson about sharing, you might give one preschooler many toys, while another has none. Ask, "How does it feel to have all of the toys? none of the toys? How can we make things fair?"
- A common cry of preschoolers is "That's not fair!" When they say this, talk with them about their feelings. Ask, "What can we do to make things more fair?" Talk about ways to treat people fairly and equally.

- Together, look at photographs of children who live in different countries. Ask, "What's different about where this child lives and where we live?" Talk with the preschooler about some of the differences and the things they have in common.
- Have a preschooler help you sort things you no longer use and donate them to a worthy cause. With your help, preschoolers can choose some of their toys to donate, too.
- Have preschoolers start a penny bank collection to give to UNICEF or a similar organization. Talk about what pennies buy. For example, through UNICEF, 2 pennies buy a pencil for a classroom and 21 pennies can buy enough penicillin to fight a child's infection. For more information, contact the U.S. Committee for UNICEF, P.O. Box 98006, Washington, DC 20077-7636; toll-free phone: 1-800-FOR-KIDS (1-800-367-5437).

RESOURCE

Common Cents New York, Inc.
500 Eighth Avenue
New York, NY 10018
Telephone: (212) 736-6437

This organization accepts donations of pennies to help children who are homeless.

- Help preschoolers throw a "picnic" for all their stuffed animals. Ask them how they would treat the animals so that the event would be fair and fun for all.
- Every preschooler has a different personality. Be sensitive to this and make an effort to spend time with children who are slow to warm up to you.

ELEMENTARY-AGE CHILDREN

- Treat children with respect. Ask for children's opinions. Listen to their ideas. Respect their suggestions.
- Choose a region of your country or a developing country for you and a child to study. Find out how people live together there. Is

there poverty? a class system? Does the culture value youth? older people? Compare the area to your own. Are your social values different or the same? What do you think is good and bad about the different values?

- Help children show their concern for people who are hungry. For example, some children ask birthday party guests not to bring presents but to bring canned food to donate to a food drive instead.

- Find out what children think about equality. Ask questions like, "Who gets treated more fairly: boys or girls? rich people or poor people? heavy people or thin people?"

- With the help of a few children, make a list of some social justice concerns (such as poverty, human rights, and so on). Show the list to a group of children and ask them to choose the issues that are most important to them. Compare how different children feel. Do they share the same concerns? Ask children to suggest ways to work on the issues that are most important to them.

- Give children hands-on experiences to help those who don't usually receive equal treatment. What can you do to help people who are physically or mentally challenged, or families who have moved from another country? Together with children, you might volunteer at a care center or help people learn to speak English.

- Help children learn about an organization before they make a donation. Children might choose to investigate groups that help animals or promote the rights of children.

- Some organizations don't accept volunteers who are younger than age 16 or 18. If this is the case in your area, find alternative ways for children to help others. Can a younger child accompany an adult volunteer? Can children work with an adult service organization? Have a child talk to a teacher or childcare program director and offer to work with younger children. It may not be easy, but children *can* find a way to help others.

ASSETS IN ACTION
Helping Others Tastes Great!

Fifth-graders in Jill Koske's class in Marquette, Michigan, have a creative way of helping other people. Twice a month, teams of students bake bread together, using recipes and ingredients their parents provide. The children deliver the bread to people at Jantzen House, a residence for homeless people.

Asset 28

FAMILY VALUES INTEGRITY

> Parents and other adults act on their convictions
> and stand up for their beliefs. As children grow,
> they begin to stand up for their beliefs.

How Search Institute defines this asset . . .

For infants: Parents act on their convictions, stand up for their beliefs, and communicate and model this in the family.

For toddlers and preschoolers: Parents act on their convictions, stand up for their beliefs, and communicate and model this in the family.

For elementary-age children: Children begin to act on their convictions and stand up for their beliefs.

ALL CHILDREN

- The asset of integrity emerges slowly in children. You probably won't see glimmers of it until the elementary-age years. Model honesty and strong moral values for children, and they'll develop these values over time.

- With other adults, talk about your beliefs and values. Vow to do the right thing and to act on what you believe. Talking about values with adults will make it easier for you to discuss values with children.

- Keep your promises. When you say you're going to do something for a child, follow through in a reasonable time frame. If something comes up and you can't keep your promise, explain what happened. Apologize for breaking your promise.
- Look at how you respond when other people don't respect your principles, values, and beliefs. Do you behave in ways that you want children to learn? If not, think about learning new ways to stand up for yourself and your convictions.
- Be true to yourself by getting in touch with who you are. For example, if you enjoy quiet times, make time in your day for solitude. Create a lifestyle that genuinely fits you. Teach children to do the same. This kind of personal honesty and understanding is the foundation for integrity.

INFANTS

- Be direct about what's right and wrong. Say things like, "It's not okay to bite people." Make your values clear.
- When an adult isn't treating an infant well, speak up and say so. Don't use language that blames. Instead, say, "The baby is crying. We need to find out what's wrong and take care of her."
- Stand up for yourself, especially when you feel your principles and values have been violated. This models integrity for infants.

TODDLERS

- Value toddlers' feelings. Work *with* their feelings instead of *against* them. People with integrity work to be in touch with their emotions and act according to their values. Begin to teach these skills to toddlers.
- When toddlers say "Mine" and "No," they're developing a strong sense of self. This is an important part of integrity. Before they can respect the belongings of others, toddlers need to understand the concept of ownership. Respect toddlers' possessions and opinions and teach them to share and respect those of others.
- Toddlers will hit, punch, grab, and poke to defend themselves—and their things. Talk with toddlers about positive

ways to defend themselves and their possessions. For example, when 2-year-old Chua has her toy snatched away from her, she jumps up, points to the toy, and tells the childcare provider, "That's mine!" When toddlers respond in a way like this, let them know you approve of their words and actions.

PRESCHOOLERS

- It's not always clear to adults how to act with integrity. When you are struggling with an integrity issue—for example, whether to speak up or stay silent—use simple terms to talk about your dilemma with preschoolers. "When you're with a group of people and you're upset with someone, sometimes it's better to stay silent and wait until later to talk to the person alone."

- Do your best to have preschoolers spend time with adults who stand up for their beliefs and act on their convictions.

- Point out when children act in ways you don't value. You might say, "When we get angry, we don't slam doors on people's fingers. It's okay to feel mad, but it's not okay to hurt someone."

- Teach children about integrity in simple ways. For example, "When someone thanks you for something you didn't do, it's important to say so. You can say, 'Thanks for thanking me, but Jared was the one who did this for you.'"

ELEMENTARY-AGE CHILDREN

- Teach children about people who model integrity (such as Helen Keller, Martin Luther King Jr., Marian Wright Edelman, and Mahatma Gandhi). Learn about the things these people did. Read their biographies. How have they made a difference?

- Ask children what they stand for—and against. Help them make a list of things. You might say, "Why are the things on your list important to you? What are some things you can do to show how you feel?" Have children save their lists. Later, if they're struggling with an issue, have them look at their list to help them decide how to act.

RESOURCE

Kids for Saving Earth (KSE)
P.O. Box 421118
Minneapolis, MN 55442
Telephone: (612) 559-1234
Email: KSEWW@aol.com

When Clinton Hill died from cancer at age 11, his family established KSE as a nonprofit organization to carry on Clint's dream of empowering children to live and act in earth-friendly ways.

- When children post "Keep Out" signs and request privacy, they're standing up for what's theirs. Respect their wishes by giving them the space they need. Help children be firm, but not harsh, with siblings and other people who don't honor their requests. In addition, teach children to recognize the signs and symbols other people use when they want privacy.

- Help a child select one value to stand up for. Together, learn more about this value and find ways for the child to make it a more important part of his life. For example, a child who chooses to stand up for honesty might create a personal "honesty pledge" stating his beliefs and then post it in a prominent place in his home.

RESOURCE

Being Your Best: Character Development for Kids 7–10 by Barbara A. Lewis (Minneapolis: Free Spirit Publishing, 2000) is a book that teaches elementary-age children ways to develop 10 traits: caring, citizenship, cooperation, fairness, forgiveness, honesty, relationships, respect, responsibility, and safety. There's also a companion book for adults, *A Leader's Guide to Being Your Best.*

- Talk about your views of public figures who act with integrity—or without it. Ask children for their opinions, too.

You might say, "Do you think it's right for teachers to go on strike? Why do you feel that way?"

- Tell children about a time when taking a stand was a hard thing for you to do. Explain how you felt before and after.
- Applaud children when they stick up for their beliefs, especially when this is difficult for them. For example, when a child befriends another child who is teased by classmates, you might say, "I see that treating people with respect is important to you. It's great that you stand up for what you believe."

RESOURCE

The Giraffe Project
P.O. Box 759
Langley, WA 98260
Telephone: (360) 221-7989
Web site: *www.positiveuniverse.com/giraffe.htm*

This organization encourages children and adults to "stick their necks out" to make the world a better place by working on problems like pollution, hunger, and violence.

Asset 29

FAMILY VALUES HONESTY

Parents and other adults model honesty
and teach children the difference
between lying and telling the truth. As children
become older, they begin to value honesty.

How Search Institute defines this asset . . .

For infants and toddlers: Parents tell the truth and convey their belief in honesty through their actions.

For preschoolers: Preschoolers learn the difference between telling the truth and lying.

For elementary-age children: Children begin to value honesty and act accordingly.

ALL CHILDREN

- It takes many years for children to learn the value of honesty. When children have honest adults in their lives, they're more likely to learn that it's important to be truthful.

- When a child lies, stay calm. Talk about better ways the child could have acted. Ask, "How could you do things differently next time?" Say, "It's not okay to lie."

- Use simple words to talk about what being truthful means. For example, say, "Part of being honest is facing what you've done wrong. It's okay to admit that you've made a mistake and apologize if you need to."

INFANTS

- Sow the seeds of honesty by making sure the people who interact with infants are honest with themselves and other people. When you're around an infant, be truthful. For example, when an adult is late for a play date, talk about it in front of the baby. Be direct, assertive, and polite: "We're glad to see you. We were expecting you at three o'clock."
- Infants watch their siblings for cues on how to act. Teach an infant's siblings to tell the truth.
- Caring for an infant can be exhausting. Be honest with yourself and with others. When you're tired, admit it. Take a break if you need it.
- Think about how comfortable you are with infants. What can you handle? What's too much for you? Talk honestly about your feelings with your partner, a friend you trust, or a professional. Don't be afraid to ask for advice and guidance. Your own personal honesty is the foundation for modeling and nurturing this value.

TODDLERS

- Toddlers have trouble distinguishing between what's honest and what's dishonest. Point out the difference to toddlers now—and many times during their childhood years. For example, when a toddler with cracker crumbs on his mouth and hands says, "I didn't eat the cracker," calmly point out that you see the cracker crumbs and that it's important to tell the truth.
- Sometimes toddlers will say "No" to whatever you ask them— even things you're sure they'd really like to do. ("Do you want to play a game?" "No." "Are you ready to go to the park?" "No.") A toddler who answers in this way isn't being dishonest.

She's practicing being a separate person. Be patient and ask again in a few minutes.

- Admit when you've been dishonest around a toddler. For example, say, "I'm sorry I told you the cookies are all gone when they really aren't. I think it would be better if you had a healthy snack, like an apple, instead of a cookie."

- Praise toddlers when they're truthful. Thank them for telling you things that were hard for them to talk about. Say, "Thanks for letting me know that you lost your mittens at the park. I'm glad you were honest and told me what happened."

PRESCHOOLERS

- Talk with preschoolers about the difference between lying and telling the truth. Then role-play situations where preschoolers can choose to be truthful or not. Say, "Imagine that you broke your father's favorite CD. I'll pretend to be your father and ask you what happened." Talk about what happens after someone tells the truth—or a lie.

 DID YOU KNOW?

Lying is very common with 3- to 5-year-olds, says the American Academy of Pediatrics. Preschoolers may lie because they've gotten swept up with their imagination, they're afraid of getting punished, or they're imitating adults. Before confronting a child about lying, take time to consider why the child has lied.

Source: *Caring for Your Baby and Young Child: Birth to Age 5* by the American Academy of Pediatrics (New York: Bantam, 1998), p. 373.

- When you know a preschooler has lied, point it out. Explain why it's wrong to lie. Talk about how important it is to be honest. Don't ask the child if he's told you the truth—this could lead him to tell another lie. Say, "It can be hard to tell the truth sometimes. It's okay for you to make a mistake, but it isn't okay for you to lie about what happened."

- Keep your expectations realistic. For example, when a preschooler goes to a party, don't say, "You'll have such a good time" or "I know it'll be fun!" You *don't* know if this will be true. Instead, say something like, "I hope you'll have fun at the party. I want to hear all about it later."

- It can take careful thought to be honest with preschoolers. A preschooler may ask, "Can we go to the park?" If you reply, "Let's go this afternoon" but change your mind when afternoon rolls around, the child will learn that she can't rely on what you say. Unless you're positive about your afternoon plans, it's safer and more honest to respond, "Maybe we can go this afternoon" or, "I don't know yet, but I'll think about it."

ELEMENTARY-AGE CHILDREN

- Focus on the positive. When children are honest, let them know you approve. Assume that children tell the truth most of the time. Believe their stories, but ask a lot of questions.

- When you realize you've lied or stretched the truth, admit it. Explain why you acted this way. Apologize. Say, "I'm sorry I didn't tell the truth. I'm feeling really crabby and I spoke without thinking." (This shows children that honesty is the way to fix a mistake. It's also helpful for children to hear because they may not realize it's easier to lie when they're tired or under pressure.)

RESOURCE

Teaching Your Children Values by Linda Eyre and Richard Eyre (New York: Fireside, 1993) includes age-appropriate ideas for helping children age 2 and older develop many positive values including honesty, justice, and respect.

- Avoid labeling children. A child who's labeled will meet your expectations—or lack of them. For example, a child labeled a "liar" may think of herself that way, or a child who's called a "good boy" may be afraid to talk about something bad that might harm his image. Instead, focus on the specific behavior that concerns you: "It was wrong to lie to your teacher. You need to tell the truth." "I'm glad you were honest about what happened."

- Understand that children sometimes lie when they feel stressed. When this happens, talk about things the child might do to cope with stress (like take a walk, shoot baskets, write in a journal, or talk to an adult about the problem).

- Encourage children to tell the truth, even after they've lied. For example, when you think a child has lied, say something like, "It's hard to believe that your teacher let Linda slug you. Are you sure that's what happened?" Tell the child you won't be angry if he "comes clean."

- Talk about "stretching the truth" and telling "little white lies" and why people do these things. Say, "Have you ever told a lie so you wouldn't hurt someone's feelings? How could you be honest instead?" Help children find ways to be both honest and caring. For example, if a child receives a birthday gift she already has, she doesn't need to strain the truth by saying, "It's just what I wanted" or lie with, "I've been wanting one of these!" To be sincere and honest, she can simply say, "Thank you."

- Keep your eye on the newspaper for stories about people who choose to lie or tell the truth. When it's appropriate, talk about these stories with children.

Asset 30

FAMILY VALUES RESPONSIBILITY

Parents and other adults model personal responsibility. Children learn that actions affect others. As they grow, children accept and take responsibility for their decisions and actions.

How Search Institute defines this asset . . .

For infants and toddlers: Parents accept and take personal responsibility.

For preschoolers: Preschoolers learn that their actions affect other people.

For elementary-age children: Children begin to accept and take personal responsibility for age-appropriate tasks.

ALL CHILDREN

- Part of being responsible is being available. Be there when children need you.
- Talk to parents about what it means to be responsible. How can they model responsibility for children? For example, parents might talk about their responsibilities as they do them. "Paying the bills is one of the things I do to be responsible."
- Keep track of your daily responsibilities with to-do lists or another method that works for you. Teach children ways that they can be responsible, too.

- Responsibilities can be overwhelming for young children. Help children find ways to break down bigger tasks into smaller parts. For example, rather than expect a 5-year-old to clean her room, work with her to do this. As you do, help her find tasks that will help her progress: putting toys in a toy box, placing books on a shelf, putting dirty laundry in a basket, and so on. As children grow, they can gradually take on more of the responsibility. Work with them each step of the way until they're ready to "go it alone."

INFANTS

- Keep infants near you when you're doing simple tasks. For example, some adults fold laundry while a baby snuggles with them in a child carrier.
- Let infants play with the tools they'll use to take care of their responsibilities when they're older. For example, an infant might chew on a washcloth in the bathtub—eventually, she'll learn how to use it to wash herself.
- Talk out loud as you care for an infant. For example, say, "I take off your diaper, then I clean you up. Then I put a clean diaper on you." This teaches children that some responsibilities have several steps.

TODDLERS

- Teach toddlers how to behave responsibly. Help them learn to brush their teeth before going to bed and remember to turn off the lights when they leave a room. Toddlers will need plenty of positive reinforcement to do these things on their own, so be patient. Thank toddlers when they're responsible, even if they don't do the task perfectly.
- Toddlers will make it clear when they want to do things on their own. When they're able, let them put on their own shirt or socks.
- Toddlers learn responsibility by doing. Give toddlers simple responsibilities, such as pushing wet clothes into the dryer or putting napkins on the table before a meal. Have them put their toys away. Add more responsibilities as they grow older.

- Do responsible things side by side with toddlers. For example, pick up and put away crayons or books together.

Preschoolers

- If a preschooler won't do what you ask, find out what's wrong. He may be tired or hungry, or want some attention. If this is the case, meet the child's needs, then have him take care of his responsibility.

RESOURCE

Raising a Responsible Child by Elizabeth M. Ellis (New York: Birch Lane Press, 1995) suggests ways to help children (from preschoolers to young adults) develop responsibility.

- Preschoolers often need to be reminded to be responsible. For example, you'll probably need to tell a child many times to pick up her toys. Be patient. Learning responsibility takes time.
- Teach preschoolers ways to take care of themselves. For example, they can be in charge of washing and drying their hands after using the toilet.
- Preschoolers sometimes take shortcuts with their responsibilities. Talk about why it's important to complete responsibilities carefully.
- Ask preschoolers questions about their responsibilities. Help them make connections between what they're doing and why it's important. You might ask, "Why do we match socks instead of just mixing them all in the drawer?"

Elementary-Age Children

- When children don't meet their responsibilities, use logical consequences. For example, if a child gets an allowance for cleaning her bedroom, make sure the room is clean before she gets any money.

? DID YOU KNOW?

Parents and other adults need to give children meaningful, age-appropriate activities to enhance personal responsibility. Guiding a child to fulfill a responsibility is quite different from giving the child the entire responsibility with no assistance. For example, children in the early-elementary grades might be overwhelmed with the sole responsibility of doing a school project. However, the parent can work side by side with the child. As the child grows older and can handle more responsibility, the parent can gradually shift responsibility to the child.

Source: E.E. Maccoby, "Middle Childhood in the Context of the Family," in *Development During Middle Childhood: The Years Six to Twelve,* edited by W.A. Collins (Washington, DC: National Academy of Sciences Press, 1984), pp. 184–239.

- Keep track of how well children complete their responsibilities. Answer any questions they have and help them when they need it. If a child is responsible for caring for a family pet, be certain that the child is doing a good job so the animal is well treated.

- Let children choose what household jobs they'll be responsible for. If children have chosen their chores, they're more likely to do them willingly.

- Give children a list of regular, clearly defined tasks to do, such as making the bed, packing their lunch, and washing their hair.

- Let children find out what happens when they don't take care of their responsibilities. For example, if a child forgets to clear his place after dinner, the dirty dishes may be waiting for him at breakfast.

- Talk about how being responsible shows people that you're dependable, hard-working, and trustworthy. Point out how responsibility affects other people.

ASSETS IN ACTION
A School-Community Partnership

The entrance hallway in one Carver County, Minnesota, school has unique decorations—eight flags to represent the eight values identified by the community's asset-building initiative: citizenship, environmentalism, generosity, human worth and dignity, integrity, learning, respect for others, and responsibility. At the same school the hallways, gym, lunchroom, and offices are named after these eight values. The values are also posted in the classrooms to provide a common language to guide behavior. Every week, students in the school are recognized for demonstrating one or more of the eight values. In 1997, the Carver County District 112 school board chairman signed a "Community Values Week Proclamation," putting in place an annual week-long promotion of the eight community values.

Asset 31

FAMILY VALUES
HEALTHY LIFESTYLE

Parents and other adults model, monitor, and teach healthy habits. Children learn to take care of their bodies, which includes developing healthy sexual attitudes.

How Search Institute defines this asset . . .

For infants and toddlers: Parents love children, setting the foundation for infants and toddlers to develop healthy attitudes and beliefs about relationships. Parents model, monitor, and teach the importance of good health habits, and provide good nutritional choices and adequate rest and playtime.

For preschoolers: Parents and other adults model, monitor, and teach the importance of good health habits. Preschoolers begin to learn healthy sexual attitudes and beliefs as well as respect for others.

For elementary-age children: Children begin to value good health habits and learn healthy sexual attitudes and beliefs as well as respect for others.

ALL CHILDREN

- Examine your own beliefs, values, and views about health and sexuality. What do you want children to learn from you? Find ways to get these messages across. For example, you might point out to children that the family eats vegetables and foods with protein before eating dessert. Teach children that *they* can

217

decide who touches them and when. Before taking your child's hand, ask, "May I hold hands with you?"

- Model happy and loving relationships. Children who see adults hugging and kissing as part of a committed relationship are more likely to grow up with healthy sexual attitudes.
- Limit the television programs children watch and the sites they visit on the Internet. Shows and sites with graphic sex or violence aren't appropriate for children. Find more suitable programs instead—or turn off the television and the computer and do something together.

RESOURCE

Flight of the Stork by Anne C. Bernstein (Indianapolis, IN: Perspectives Press, 1994) explains what children understand about sex and reproduction at each age and how to encourage children to embrace healthy lifestyle habits and develop restraint.

INFANTS

- Love infants unconditionally. Love helps infants develop healthy attitudes about themselves, their bodies, and other people, which are the basis for mature sexual attitudes and behaviors.
- Give infants nutritious foods. Hold off introducing children to sugar for as long as you can. Some families choose to give children their first taste of sugar on their first birthday—in their birthday cake. Other families wait until the child discovers sugar on her own. Either way, limit the amount of sugar in an infant's diet.
- Make sure infants get plenty of rest every day. Follow a newborn's sleep patterns for the first several months before expecting him to settle into a routine.
- Play with infants every day. Have fun with them. Show them that play is an important part of a healthy lifestyle.
- Create a daily personal care routine for an infant. Brush an infant's new teeth and let her play with the toothbrush. Help

her get used to the concept of brushing and keeping her teeth clean. Comment on the habits you want to teach: "Brushing our teeth helps them grow strong."

TODDLERS

- Hugging and holding toddlers shows that you love and accept them. This helps them develop a strong, healthy sense of self.
- Introduce nutritious foods to toddlers. Expect their interest in eating (and in trying new foods) to rise and fall.
- A well-rested toddler is happy, ready to learn, and fun to be around. Do your best to set a regular naptime and bedtime schedule for a toddler.
- Many toddlers enjoy taking off their diaper or clothes. (They're usually less interested in putting them on.) When they're at home, let them run around in the nude once in a while.
- Let toddlers know that taking baths, combing hair, and brushing teeth are important activities that can be fun, too. Smile at a toddler and laugh together as you teach him to take care of himself.
- Keep a close eye on toddlers who are learning to use the toilet. Toilet training takes time, so be patient. Be prepared to repeat instructions, give reminders, and clean up after accidents. Keep a positive attitude and let toddlers know you love them no matter what.

PRESCHOOLERS

- Respect preschoolers' privacy, and teach them to respect the privacy of others. You might say, "Bathroom time is private time. If the bathroom door is closed, knock and ask if someone's in there before you open the door."
- Talk with preschoolers about how they can take care of themselves. Say, "It's important for people to eat three healthy meals every day and get plenty of rest and exercise. Can you name some healthy foods?"
- You and a preschooler may not agree on what clothing—or lack of clothing—is appropriate. Set clear guidelines about

how children should dress in public and at home. "It's fun to wear your socks on your hands at home. But when we're going shopping, you need to put them on your feet."

- Use the correct names for body parts. It's important for children to learn that you're comfortable talking about the human body and sexuality.

- When preschoolers ask questions about sexuality, give honest and simple answers.

 ## DID YOU KNOW?

When children are exposed to healthy lifestyles and healthy sexual attitudes, they're more likely to make these things a part of their lives. As they grow, children will gradually learn to use restraint and avoid unhealthy and risky behaviors. Teenagers who've been raised in an environment where healthy lifestyles are important are less likely to engage in early sexual intercourse or use alcohol or other drugs.

Source: A.C. Petersen and N. Leffert, "Developmental Issues Influencing Guidelines for Adolescent Health Research: A Review." *Journal of Adolescent Health* 17 (1995).

ELEMENTARY-AGE CHILDREN

- Keep a strong connection to children. Love and support them in ways they appreciate. For example, some children are embarrassed when you give them a hug and kiss in front of their friends. Instead, you might write the child a short "I think you're special" note and tuck it in her lunchbox or under her pillow.

- Use simple words to talk with children about your sexual values. For example, say, "I don't let anyone kiss me unless I want to be kissed." "It's up to *me* if I want a hug. And it's up to *you* if you want one, too."

- Help children make healthy choices about eating, sleeping, bathing, and grooming. You might ask, "Would you like an apple or some grapes for dessert today?"
- As children are ready to learn about sex and sexuality, give them accurate, appropriate information. Don't assume they'll learn everything they need to know in school or from their friends. Give them information a piece at a time, and be prepared to answer questions.
- Discuss how characters on television and in the movies relate to each other. Talk about who's respectful, loving, and empathetic—and who's not.
- Talk with children about gender roles. Let them know that it's perfectly fine for girls to play with trucks and for boys to play with dolls. Say, "Girls and boys are different, but that doesn't mean they have to do different things." Explain that it's okay for all kids—boys and girls alike—to be both gentle and caring and strong and assertive.
- When children make inappropriate remarks about sexuality and body parts, stay calm. Let children know what's not acceptable, but don't reward them by giving their comments a lot of attention.

ASSETS IN ACTION
Caring for Children

Public health nurses in Kodiak, Alaska, talk to parents about asset building during well-child exams. Asset building "focuses on positive, simple, everyday actions that any of us can do whether we have children in our lives as family members or extended family," says Becky Judd of the Alaska Public Health Division.

MORE IDEAS FOR BUILDING THE POSITIVE VALUES ASSETS

IDEAS FOR PARENTS

- Talk about your values. Put them into practice.
- Make helping others a family activity. For example, if a neighbor is injured or ill, make get-well cards together. Bake cookies and take them over. Offer to do some laundry or take care of a pet.
- What social concerns are most important to you and your children? Choose one issue for your family to work on each year. Find ways for every family member to help make a difference.
- Make honesty an important family value. When your children lie, say, "People in this family tell the truth." Give children a chance to be honest.
- Find out what values were important to your ancestors—and why. What family values have been passed through the generations of your family? Ask older relatives to talk with children about events that shaped the family's beliefs.
- Talk with your children about the values of characters you see on television and in the movies. Ask questions like, "What's important to that person? What do you think the person values?" Have children watch for characters who are caring and responsible or have other important values.

IDEAS FOR CHILDCARE PROVIDERS

- Be clear about what kind of behavior is and isn't appropriate. Explain why. Young children can develop positive values when they have clear boundaries. For example, say, "Thank you for telling me that you spilled the glue. We'll clean up the mess together."
- Help children learn values through play. For example, children learn about caring when they get a hug from another child.

Teach children about values by modeling them and promoting them, not by setting rigid rules. Treat children with respect, and they'll follow your lead.

• Give children lots of chances to make choices. When children make decisions, they learn to think things through and develop their own sense of right and wrong.

• Children need nutritious food, plenty of rest, and lots of love to help them develop a healthy sense of self and positive attitudes about their bodies. Make sure they're getting what they need.

IDEAS FOR EDUCATORS

• Some people argue that schools shouldn't teach values because not everyone can agree on which values are most important. However, there are a few positive values—such as honesty, caring, and responsibility—that most people agree on. Teach children about these values, and help children learn that the values we share make us better people and create a better society.

• Send thank-you notes to class visitors. After a field trip, have students send notes to people they visited. With younger children, create a group thank-you letter and have each child sign it.

• Make a list of classroom responsibilities that students might have. Post the list on the wall, and assign each responsibility to one student. Give students a chance to switch jobs and try new things throughout the year.

• Plan activities where children can care for and support others. For example, students can mentor each other or younger children. They can plant a school garden (outdoors, or indoors in pots) and donate the produce to hungry people.

• Get students involved in service-learning projects. Children might create their own bicycle-safety campaign. They could research the issue, create a flyer and distribute it around the area, and write a short play to perform for other classes. Afterward, talk together about what it was like to help others. Did the children make a difference? Did other people learn from them? Create ways for them to evaluate their experience.

Ask, "How well did this work? What would you have done differently? What will you do next time?"

- Have students make an equality bulletin board. On the board, students can post pictures and short biographies of people who worked for equal rights. Add to the profiles throughout the year. Create other bulletin boards for values like honesty and responsibility.

IDEAS FOR HEALTH-CARE PROFESSIONALS

- Respect the children and adults who are in your care. Adults who bring in sick children often feel afraid and alone. Listen to their concerns. Show them that you want to help.

- Provide low-cost or free health-care services for low-income families. Support free clinics in your area—and volunteer at them, if you can.

- Speak out about children's rights in your community. Other people respect you in your professional role and will listen to what you have to say.

- Parents of a chronically ill child have a lot of responsibilities. Support them as they take care of their child and learn more about the child's illness. Tell them about magazine articles, books, TV shows, or Web sites that talk about the illness. Be available for after-hours phone consultations. Ask what parents are doing to take care of themselves, too. Encourage them to find ways to take an occasional break and renew themselves.

- Take a look at your facilities and programs. How can children and families help improve them? Families might volunteer to visit hospitalized children, paint examination rooms, and tutor children who need long-term medical care.

IDEAS FOR CONGREGATIONAL LEADERS

- Find ways for children and families to help others. For example, work together to clean up a neighborhood park.

- Take a careful look at the children's activities and programs your congregation provides. How can you use these to teach positive values?

- Declare this "The Year of Values" for your congregation. Focus on the specific values that are important to your faith tradition. Have children make posters about values to hang in your facilities. Sponsor workshops and seminars where parents, care providers, and teachers can learn effective ways to teach values to children.
- Develop a series of services about positive values. Include readings and songs about these values. Talk about them in small study groups. After the series is finished, have an event where all ages can gather to celebrate the congregation's values.

IDEAS FOR EMPLOYERS

- Find ways to show you care about employees' children. For example, some companies give free car seats to new parents, or graduation gifts to children when they finish high school.
- Set fair and equitable family policies. For example, make paid parental leave available to parents who adopt a child.
- Help employees find creative ways to handle their family responsibilities. Let workers vary their schedules now and then to attend a childcare program or a soccer game. Allow employees to use their sick leave to take care of sick children.
- Create policies that help employees help each other. For example, some employers let workers donate unused paid time off to other employees who have chronically ill children or face emergency situations.

IDEAS FOR LIBRARIANS

- At storytime, read books about positive values. Have storytellers dress up like characters from these books. For example, an adult could dress as Pinocchio and talk about how the little boy's nose grew or shrank as he lied or told the truth.
- Have a group of children create a puppet show based on a children's book about positive values. The children can perform their show at the library and at local schools.
- April 30 is National Honesty Day. Plan special activities and read books about honesty to celebrate the day. Invite an author who writes about honesty to speak at your library.

- Honor children who do caring activities in your community. Post photographs of the children and stories about their activities. Create a scrapbook of these materials and make it part of your library's collection.
- Have a poetry-writing workshop for children, with positive values as the theme.

RESOURCE

The Story of Ruby Bridges by Robert Coles (New York: Scholastic, 1995) tells about a 6-year-old girl who displayed both courage and compassion when she became the first black child to attend an all-white elementary school in 1960.

IDEAS FOR COMMUNITY LEADERS

- Gather concerned adults to create a list of your community's shared values. Talk about ways to strengthen these values and make them known to everyone in the community.
- What can your community do to help people in need? With the help of a school, business, or community organization, sponsor a coat drive, toy drive, or another project that helps others.
- Have families, schools, congregations, and children's organizations (such as scout troops) help out with neighborhood rehabilitation projects.
- Create a children's rights commission in your community. Children with strong leadership skills can meet to talk about problems the community's children face and suggest solutions.
- With the help of the police department, create asset-building programs for young offenders. Help young people learn to take responsibility for their actions.

We encourage you to photocopy this page (set the image size at 125 percent), cut out the "Ideas for Children," and share them with a child you know.

IDEAS FOR CHILDREN: BUILDING YOUR OWN POSITIVE VALUES ASSETS

- Watch for people who could use your help. Do what you can to help them.

- What do you stand for? What's important to you? Let other people know what you believe.

- Make a promise to yourself to tell the truth. It can be hard to be honest, but it's worth it.

- Let other people know that they can count on you. Have a backup plan ready in case you have a problem following through.

- Take care of your body. Eat healthy foods and get plenty of rest and exercise.

- Show people you care. When you meet someone, smile!

- When something isn't fair, speak up. Your feelings and ideas are important.

THE SOCIAL
COMPETENCIES ASSETS

It takes time for children to learn to relate to other people in positive ways. The more opportunities children have to experiment and practice, the better they'll get. Children learn how to act from observing the people around them. As children grow older, they're able to apply the skills they've seen others use and begin to handle social situations on their own. When they're socially competent, children can cope with the many choices, challenges, and opportunities they face in life.

The social competencies category includes five developmental assets for children from birth through age 11:

The Social Competencies Assets

Asset 32: Planning and Decision Making

Asset 33: Interpersonal Skills

Asset 34: Cultural Competence

Asset 35: Resistance Skills

Asset 36: Peaceful Conflict Resolution

When Search Institute surveyed 6th graders, they found that children experience some of the social competencies assets more than others. Here are the percentages of these children who reported the assets in their lives:*

Asset 32: Planning and Decision Making	**31%**
Asset 33: Interpersonal Competence	**47%**
Asset 34: Cultural Competence	**41%**
Asset 35: Resistance Skills	**49%**
Asset 36: Peaceful Conflict Resolution	**54%**

---

*Some of the asset names in the survey of 6th graders are different from those relating to younger children. The survey's asset names are the names that apply to older children and teens. The asset names in *What Young Children Need to Succeed* take into account developmental and situational differences of young children. See pages 3–5 for further information about asset language.

Asset 32

PLANNING AND DECISION MAKING

Parents and other adults help children learn how to make choices as appropriate. Preschoolers and elementary-age children begin to plan ahead and solve problems.

How Search Institute defines this asset . . .

For infants and toddlers: Parents make all safety and care decisions for children and model safe behavior. As children become more independently mobile, parents allow them to make simple choices.

For preschoolers: Preschoolers begin to make simple choices, solve simple problems, and develop simple plans at age-appropriate levels.

For elementary-age children: Children begin to learn how to plan ahead and make choices at appropriate developmental levels.

ALL CHILDREN

- Think about your own planning and decision-making skills. Build on your strengths and work on your weaknesses. Model these skills for children. For example, use things-to-do lists and planning calendars.
- Be patient with children as they learn to make decisions. Let them consider their options without rushing them to choose.
- Children may not always understand what their choices are. For example, a child may grab a handful of snacks when you've said

he can have one. Explain that he can choose one treat and leave the rest.

INFANTS

- Make healthy decisions about an infant's care, nutrition, and daily schedule. Talk to infants about the choices you make for them. Say, "Because it's raining, we're not going to the park today. We'll stay inside, where it's warm and dry."
- Make sure the environment is always safe. For example, never leave a baby alone on a changing table, even if you think she can't roll off.
- Be prepared when you travel with an infant. Bring along all the essentials you'll need to take care of the baby, including bottles, diapers, extra clothes, and a few favorite toys.
- Learn how an infant communicates his likes and dislikes. For example, a baby may spit out sweet potatoes to let you know he doesn't like them. Respect his decision and give him something he likes instead. Let him decide when he's ready for more by waiting for him to turn to you before you feed him another spoonful.

TODDLERS

- Give toddlers two equally appealing choices whenever you can. For example, say, "Would you like to drink orange juice or grape juice with your snack today?"
- It's important to respect a toddler's decisions, but sometimes this just isn't practical. Explain your reasoning. ("I don't think it's a good idea for you to play in the snow without your snowsuit on. You'll get cold.") Be firm but kind.
- Create decision-making games for toddlers. They might like a game where they choose whether to draw with a blue crayon or a green crayon or whether to sleep in polka-dot pajamas or striped ones.
- If you ask a toddler a question, make sure you're prepared to accept all the possible answers. For example, instead of asking a child if she's ready for bed, you might say, "It's time for bed. Would you like one bedtime story, or two?"

DID YOU KNOW?

Practice helps children make better decisions. Research shows that 3- to 5-year-olds solved problems better if they had worked on a similar problem with a parent in the past.

Source: Lisa S. Freund, "Maternal Regulation of Children's Problem-solving Behavior and Its Impact on Children's Performance." *Child Development* 61 (1990).

PRESCHOOLERS

- Help preschoolers make decisions. For example, give them a choice between two outfits. If children choose their own clothes, don't worry if they wear things that don't go together.

- Teach preschoolers to plan ahead. Help them choose appropriate toys and activities to bring on a long trip. Talk about things they can do to have fun when they're visiting relatives.

- Draw simple pictures showing the events of a preschooler's day. You might draw a toothbrush, a bowl of cereal, and a shopping cart. Explain, "After you wake up tomorrow, you'll brush your teeth and eat breakfast, then we'll go to the supermarket."

- Preschoolers sometimes get bored at playtime. When this happens, pull out some toys or activities they haven't played with lately and let them choose what to do next. This gives them practice making decisions and builds their confidence.

- As a special treat, give preschoolers the power to choose how to spend an afternoon. They might want to go to the library, play at the park, or visit a grandparent. Go along with whatever they decide.

- When they're scared or overwhelmed, preschoolers need adults to make decisions for them. Turn off the television if a child is watching something inappropriate. Step in and separate children who are hitting or kicking. Help an overexcited child calm down by reading or singing to him or having him listen to quiet music.

ELEMENTARY-AGE CHILDREN

- Teach children to break down large homework assignments into smaller, more manageable pieces. Help children plan to complete the project over a few days or a week. (When children get used to doing this, they can plan on their own.)
- Children can learn to take care of their responsibilities before doing things they enjoy. You could say, "You might want to take care of your chores now. You'll enjoy the game more if you know you don't have to clean your room after you play."
- Some decisions or plans can have many steps. Help children consider all of these steps and remind them about things they may have overlooked. For example, if a child needs to buy a gift for a friend's birthday, talk about what kinds of toys the friend likes. Set a budget and a timeline. Find several options, then pick the best one.

RESOURCE

The Life-Smart Kid: Teaching Your Child to Use Good Judgment in Every Situation by Lawrence J. Greene (Rocklin, CA: Prima Publishing, 1995) offers practical ways to help children develop decision-making skills.

- Talk to children about how they make decisions. Do they act on impulse, or do they think things through carefully? Teach them some decision-making steps to help them when you're not around.
- Some children have trouble with decisions in a certain area. If this is the case, give them clear boundaries and guidelines to improve their decision-making skills. For instance, if a child has frequent fights with another child, keep the children apart for a few days. Talk to each child about how to resolve conflicts in a positive way. Then let them spend a few minutes together, with close supervision. Gradually increase their time together and decrease the supervision as they learn to get along.

- Give children tools to help them make decisions. They can make schedules and note plans on a calendar or keep track of their assignments and projects in a notebook.

ASSETS IN ACTION
Building Essential Skills

At St. Luke Presbyterian Church in Minnetonka, Minnesota, the first Saturday in December is a special day. At the congregation's annual gift-making workshop, children in grades 1 through 6 make and wrap bird feeders, door stops, tree ornaments, stationery, and many other gifts. Children plan, make decisions, and build relationships with the adults who help and guide them as they make the presents they've chosen to work on. Children give the gifts to parents, siblings, grandparents, aunts, and uncles. They enjoy making the gifts and surprising the receivers on Christmas.

Asset 33

INTERPERSONAL SKILLS

Parents and other adults respond to children's feelings and model positive interactions with others. They help children to express their feelings in appropriate ways and learn to respect the feelings of others.

How Search Institute defines this asset . . .

For infants: Parents model positive, constructive interactions with other people. Parents accept and are responsive to how infants express their feelings, seeing those expressions as cues to infants' needs.

For toddlers: Parents model positive, constructive interactions with other people. Parents accept and are responsive to how toddlers use actions and words to express their feelings, seeing those expressions as cues to toddlers' needs.

For preschoolers: Preschoolers play and interact with other children and adults. They freely express their feelings and learn to put these feelings into words. Parents and other adults model and teach empathy.

For elementary-age children: Children interact with adults and children and can make friends. Children express and articulate feelings in appropriate ways and empathize with others.

ALL CHILDREN

- Express your feelings openly and respectfully. Children learn about emotions—and how to handle them—by watching the adults around them.

- Building a child's interpersonal skills will also teach her how to care about others. For example, take a child with you when you help a neighbor with yardwork. As you work, include the child in conversation as well as in the task at hand.

- People with strong interpersonal skills are assertive and can solve problems in peaceful ways. (See Asset 36: Peaceful Conflict Resolution and Asset 37: Personal Power for some ways to build these skills in children.) Model these abilities for children.

INFANTS

- Be loving and warm toward infants. Show them that it's important for people to take care of each other.

- Infants usually spend most of their time with adults. Think of yourself as an infant's best friend. Say, "I really like you. You're a very special friend." Talk about the things friends do for each other.

- Infants love to watch and try to touch each other. Keep an eye on infants as they spend time together. Notice caring touches ("It's nice to see you being gentle") and distract infants if they get rough.

- React matter-of-factly when an infant screams. He's trying a new way to communicate and showing his independence. This usually happens when an infant is 8 or 9 months old.

- Separation anxiety—becoming upset when parents leave—is a normal part of development and learning about the differences between people. According to the American Academy of Pediatrics, separation anxiety typically peaks between 10 and 18 months of age and generally fades during the last half of the second year of life. Reassure the infant by saying, "I know you don't want me to go, but you'll be safe here at childcare. I have to go to work now, and I'll be back later to take you home."

TODDLERS

- Pay attention to the words and actions toddlers use to express their feelings. Show them how to share their emotions in appropriate ways. "I can see that you feel sad about something. Let's talk about it." "I'm glad you're so happy. Let's go outside so you'll have more room to jump up and down!"

- Toddlers are at their best when they're fed and rested. A comfortable, happy toddler will get along better with others.

- When toddlers throw tantrums, try to stay calm. Hold them and talk to them gently while they slowly relax.

- Toddlers may show affection for others in awkward ways. For example, a child may kiss another child on the back of the head. Acknowledge these gestures without correcting children—after all, it's the thought that counts. "Joey wants you to know he cares about you. Kissing your head is his way of telling you this."

- Let toddlers know that it isn't okay for them to hurt others. Tell and show them what to do instead. "If you're mad, use your words to tell me about how you feel."

PRESCHOOLERS

- Teach children the names for emotions. Look at a book or magazine together and talk about what the people in the pictures might be feeling. You might say, "That girl is learning how to ride a bike. She might feel nervous or excited. Do you know what it feels like to be nervous or excited?"

- Be sympathetic when a preschooler's feelings are hurt. Talk about what happened and help the preschooler understand the other person's point of view. For example, if a child is rejected by a playmate, you could say, "Maybe Deon wanted to play alone today. Do *you* ever want to play alone?"

- Some preschoolers have trouble losing a game graciously. Acknowledge their feelings, but encourage them to be good sports and try again.

- Teach preschoolers that other people have feelings, too. You might say, "How do you think Antonia felt when you yelled at her? How do you feel when someone yells at you?"

- Play fun games with preschoolers. Simple games like hide-and-seek teach children how to get along with other people.
- Young children "play pretend" to help them process things they've seen or experienced. Watching their play can show you if they're struggling with a particular problem. For example, you may want to talk to a child about ways to be a friend if he has his stuffed animals order each other around.

ELEMENTARY-AGE CHILDREN

- Help children learn how much fun it can be to be part of a team. Sign children up for a community soccer league or let them play kickball with other neighborhood children.
- If other children won't play with a child, find out why. Talk to the excluded child about her feelings and help her find ways to solve the problem. Don't guess—ask.
- Increase children's "feelings vocabulary." Teach children words they can use to describe their feelings more precisely. For example, a child may feel pleased, excited, content, or ecstatic instead of just happy.
- As they get older, children's relationships with members of the opposite sex will change. They may hold hands and hug each other, or tease each other and squeal about "boy germs" or "girl germs." Let children handle these relationships in their own way, but make sure they're behaving appropriately.

RESOURCE

International Society of Friendship and Good Will
412 Cherry Hills Drive
Bakersfield, CA 93309-7902
Telephone: (661) 833-9133

Each year, this organization sponsors Peace, Friendship, and Good Will Week the last seven days in October. For complete information, send $1 to cover shipping and handling costs.

- Teach children the messages their bodies send. You might cross your arms, lean back in a chair, and ask, "What does how I'm sitting tell you about how I'm feeling?" Take turns sending and receiving body language messages.
- Have children talk about what makes a good friend. Remind them that if they're good friends, people will want to be friends with them.

ASSETS IN ACTION
Learning About Social Competencies

Teachers at the Kentwood School District in Michigan have made asset-building lessons a part of their curriculum. Students learn about ways to build relationships and create a caring school environment. A special segment of the program, called "Who Me? Worried?" helps ease the transition between elementary school and middle school for the district's students. Young people feel more confident and secure as they enter middle school after completing the curriculum.

Asset 34

CULTURAL COMPETENCE

Parents and children know and are comfortable with people of different cultural, racial, and/or ethnic backgrounds.

How Search Institute defines this asset . . .

For infants and toddlers: Parents know and are comfortable with people of different cultural, racial, and/or ethnic backgrounds, and model this to children.

For preschoolers: Preschoolers are exposed in positive ways to information about and to people of different cultural, racial, and/or ethnic backgrounds.

For elementary-age children: Children know about and are comfortable with people of different cultural, racial, and/or ethnic backgrounds.

ALL CHILDREN

- Learn more about your own heritage and background. Celebrate the holidays, festivals, and other special days that are a part of your heritage. Find ways to include children in the festivities.

- Donate multicultural books, toys, and dolls to childcare centers, preschools, and elementary schools. If you can, donate cultural objects (like figurines or simple musical instruments) and clothing as well.

- Study the history and traditions of other cultures. Talk to children about what you learn.
- Give children books written by people of different cultures. Choose children's books with illustrations of and stories about many diverse people. Read the books together.
- Provide children with dolls and action figures that reflect many different races.
- Children learn from your example. Honestly examine your personal prejudices. Everyone has some level of prejudice. Which groups of people make you uncomfortable? Why? Think about why you respond that way and work to overcome your feelings.

RESOURCE

Southern Poverty Law Center
400 Washington Avenue
Montgomery, AL 36104
Telephone: (334) 264-0286
Web site: *www.splcentero.org/*

This nonprofit organization promotes intercultural and interracial understanding. It publishes the educational magazine *Teaching Tolerance,* which is free to educators who send a request for it on school letterhead.

INFANTS

- Decorate an infant's home with items from many different cultures. Place these objects where infants can see and enjoy them.
- Take infants along to events where they'll meet people of different cultures and backgrounds.
- Surround infants with multicultural toys and books. Talk to infants about the cultures that represent their favorite toys. Say things like, "You really like your toy panda, don't you? Pandas are rare and live in the bamboo forests of China."

- Make music from around the world a part of an infant's environment. For example, play children's music from Ireland, India, Mexico, Sweden, Israel, and Japan. There are many tapes and CDs of songs from around the world for young children. Check a children's bookstore or toy store or visit a local library for some ideas.

Toddlers

- Help toddlers enjoy who they are. Talk about and celebrate a toddler's heritage. Teach children a simple song from the culture and sing it along with them.
- Bring toddlers to cultural events and fairs. Find out about the culture's language, food, and games. Have fun learning and exploring together.
- Provide many different colors of crayons and paints for toddlers to use when they draw and paint.

 DID YOU KNOW?

"Culture" is more than the food people eat or the clothing they wear. Culture is part of what forms people's attitudes, identities, and day-to-day behavior. Culture involves music, language, literature, customs, traditions, religious beliefs, environment, history, and self-image. The different ways people meet their basic needs (for food, clothing, shelter, and companionship) may be based on their culture. Members of a cultural group share experiences that connect them to each other and shape the way they think and live.

Learning about culture helps children appreciate their own heritage while discovering that differences between cultures create an interesting world. When children appreciate other cultures, they're better able to respect and accept people who are different from themselves.

Source: *Discovering Me and My World: My Family* by Stephanie Feeney and Eva Moravcik (Circle Pines, MN: American Guidance Service, Inc., 1995).

- Toddlers sometimes make statements that embarrass adults. When a child announces loudly, "That boy has funny eyes," "That woman is white," "That man is going to have a baby," or "Why does that lady have a mustache?" stay calm. Explain that people come in different shapes, colors, and sizes. Use simple language to talk about ways people are different.

PRESCHOOLERS

- Teach preschoolers about their own ethnic, racial, and cultural heritage. Help them feel proud of who they are without feeling superior to other children. "You're proud to come from Ireland, just like your friend Kia is proud to be from Mexico."
- Eat foods from many cultures. Cook these foods at home or visit ethnic restaurants. Talk about food from other cultures that may already be part of the child's diet. For example, you might say, "Did you know that the first people to grow popcorn were Native Americans?"
- Choose children's television shows that promote diversity. Watch programs like *Mr. Rogers' Neighborhood*, *Zoboomafoo*, or *Sesame Street* together and answer any questions a preschooler might have.
- Learn simple dances from a variety of cultures. Play music and teach these dances to children.
- Talk with preschoolers about prejudice—and how harmful it is—in a simple way. You might say, "We don't judge people because of how they look or what they believe in. We care about other people and get to know them to find out what they're like."

ELEMENTARY-AGE CHILDREN

- With children, visit museum exhibits featuring works by people from many cultures. Talk about how people's cultural heritage colors their artistic expression.
- Children may ask questions about why people are different. For example, a child may wonder why another child stutters or uses a wheelchair. Answer these questions as completely as you can.

Help children feel more comfortable with people who are different from themselves.

- Don't tell or laugh at jokes that make fun of a person's race, gender, or ethnicity. Be clear that you think these jokes aren't appropriate.

- Help children connect with a pen pal from another country or culture. For assistance, contact International Pen Friends (IPF), P.O. Box 290065, Brooklyn, NY 11229; toll-free phone: 1-800-789-4988; Web site: *www.global-homebiz.com/ipf.html.*

- Learn about faith traditions together. Talk about what different groups believe. Ask children, "Why do you think some people don't like people of different religions?" Suggest that your congregation start a study group where children and adults can learn more about other traditions.

- Explore the differences within a larger ethnic group. For example, Chinese, Japanese, Malaysian, Vietnamese, Tongan, Korean, Laotian, Samoan, and other Pacific Islander groups are all sometimes labeled Asian, even though there are many cultural differences among these groups.

- Perceptions and beliefs about other people—both positive and negative—are often passed from parents to children for many generations. Talk to children about their ancestors' lives. Learn about the experiences these people had and how their beliefs changed over time. Ask children how these experiences influence their lives today.

RESOURCE

Roots & Wings
P.O. Box 19678
Boulder, CO 80308-2678
Toll-free phone: 1-800-833-1787
Web site: *rootsandwingscatalog.com*

Roots & Wings specializes in quality books to help elementary-age children understand the world and expand their horizons. Call, write, or visit their Web site to request a catalog.

Asset 35

RESISTANCE SKILLS

Parents and other adults model resistance skills and help children learn to make careful choices and avoid dangerous situations. As children mature, they learn to resist negative peer pressure.

How Search Institute defines this asset:

For infants: Parents model resistance skills through their own behavior.

For toddlers: Parents model resistance skills through their own behavior. Parents aren't overwhelmed by toddlers' needs and demonstrate appropriate resistance skills.

For preschoolers: Preschoolers are taught to resist participating in inappropriate or dangerous behavior.

For elementary-age children: Children start developing the ability to resist negative peer pressure and dangerous situations.

ALL CHILDREN

- Make the connection between resistance skills and integrity (see Asset 28: Family Values Integrity, pages 202–206). You can't have integrity if you can't say no and avoid dangerous situations. Promote both of these in children—and yourself.

- Practice your own resistance skills. How well can you say no to things? How easy is it for you to resist doing unacceptable or dangerous things? What do you do to cope with problems? Improve your skills so you're a role model for children. Get help if you need to control an unhealthy habit or addiction.

INFANTS

- Meet infants' needs in respectful ways. Listen to their feelings, even when they cry or fuss to express themselves. This helps children get in touch with their emotions, which is an important step in building resistance skills.
- Pay attention to how infants react to the world around them. When they're overstimulated, take them to a quiet, familiar place to calm down. Comfort them when they're upset. Give them plenty of time to explore toys that interest them. When they're older, the sense of safety and security they'll develop can help them withstand peer pressure.
- It's normal for infants who are 8 or 9 months old to be frightened of strangers. Be aware of this and introduce new people gently and carefully. Being respectful of babies' feelings helps them learn to trust themselves and may ultimately help them learn to respect themselves.
- Infants depend on caring adults to keep them safe and protected. Infants are too young to resist dangerous situations on their own, so adults need to do this for them. When an infant is playing with a toy with small parts, for example, an adult can remove the toy and give the child something more appropriate to play with.

TODDLERS

- When a toddler shouts "No, no, no!" she's beginning to assert herself and test her boundaries. React calmly; this tells her you hear her and shows her a calmer and more effective way to communicate. The skills she learns now will help her develop resistance skills later.
- Work *with* toddlers instead of *against* them. It's normal for toddlers to be contrary. Instead of getting in a power struggle,

gently redirect toddlers toward what you want them to do. Be patient as toddlers learn to be individuals.

- Toddlers can't stay out of dangerous situations on their own. They need adults to keep them safe and secure. Keep a close eye on toddlers and make sure their environment is free from potential hazards.

- Teach toddlers what is and isn't acceptable. Be firm. These boundaries will help children identify inappropriate behavior on their own when they get older. "When someone hits you, you don't hit back. Say 'Stop it' and find an adult to help."

PRESCHOOLERS

- It's normal for preschoolers to yell or hit as they begin to develop resistance skills. Teach them more appropriate ways to handle difficult situations. Say, "I know you're upset right now. Instead of using your fists, you can use your words to let people know how you feel."

- It's important for both girls and boys to learn how to be assertive. Sometimes children—girls in particular—are pressured to go along with things without standing up for themselves. Make sure all children have a chance to develop this important skill, which can help them resist peer pressure when they're older.

- Intense emotions can be overwhelming for a preschooler. Help a child identify and talk about his feelings so he can think clearly and act responsibly.

ELEMENTARY-AGE CHILDREN

- How do you cope with frustration or disappointment? Teach some of your favorite positive methods to children. For example, a child might do jumping jacks or count to 10 when he's frustrated. When he's disappointed, he could write or draw pictures in a journal.

- Help children consider all the possible solutions to a problem. Suggest ideas they might not have thought about. Ask questions and help them find their own solutions instead of solving the problem for them.

- Some children cheat, push others around, or cry to get what they want. Let children know these behaviors aren't acceptable. Teach children how to negotiate and make compromises. Help them learn healthier ways to assert themselves. When they're assertive, they're better able to say no to dangerous situations.

- Talk with children about ways they can resist danger. For example, depending on the circumstances, they might ignore the situation, walk away, tell a caring adult, or use humor. Have children come up with their own ideas, too. What ones do they like best? least? Why? Role-play situations where children can use their resistance skills.

- When helping children develop resistance skills, focus on the concepts they need to learn most. Teach a boisterous child to talk about her feelings before she acts on them. Show a shy child how to be confident and express his needs clearly.

- Give children a round of applause when they use resistance skills in positive ways—especially when they do this without prompting from adults.

RESOURCE

Helping Kids Learn Refusal Skills by David Wilmes (Minneapolis: Johnson Institute, 1991) gives practical advice on how to help children develop resistance skills.

Asset 36

PEACEFUL CONFLICT RESOLUTION

Parents and other adults model and help children learn how to cope with frustrations and resolve conflicts nonviolently.

How Search Institute defines this asset . . .

For infants and toddlers: Parents behave in acceptable, nonviolent ways and assist children in developing these skills by helping them solve problems when they're faced with challenging or frustrating circumstances.

For preschoolers: Parents and other adults model positive ways to resolve conflicts. Preschoolers are taught and begin to practice nonviolent, acceptable ways to deal with challenging and frustrating situations.

For elementary-age children: Children try to resolve conflicts nonviolently.

ALL CHILDREN

- Examine how you behave when you get angry or face a conflict. Do you try to understand the other person's point of view? Do you work to find a solution? Think about what children are learning from your actions.
- Children can learn violent behavior from movies, video games, and television programs, among other things. Keep a

close eye on what children are watching. Ask children questions about programs you watch together. You might say, "People laughed when that man fell down the stairs. Do you think that's funny? Tell me why."

- Give yourself time away from children to relax and take care of yourself. Taking care of a child can be exhausting. You'll handle conflict more effectively when you're calm and in control.

INFANTS

- Create a calm, nurturing environment for infants. Make sure babies hear adults solve problems in peaceful ways—not with shouting or angry words.
- Separate yourself from a baby who bites. Calmly say, "No biting." (It's *never* a good idea to bite back to "teach the baby a lesson.") Be firm and loving.
- Older siblings may hurt an infant, unintentionally or on purpose. Let all children know that violence of any kind isn't acceptable.
- Caring for an infant can be difficult at times. If you feel angry or frustrated, take a break. Let someone else watch the baby for a while, or put the baby in a safe place (like a crib) while you take a minute to relax.

TODDLERS

- Aggressiveness can be part of a toddler's nature. Help the child find better, more positive ways to deal with her feelings. For example, she may draw or paint an "angry picture" and then describe her feelings to you.
- Let toddlers know you're pleased when they cooperate. For example, say, "I like to see you working together on your sand castle."
- When a toddler misbehaves, be firm. Say, "I know you want a snack, but it isn't snacktime now. Please don't yell. We'll have our snack after we finish the laundry." If you give in, toddlers learn that negative behavior can get them what they want.
- Sometimes toddlers act up because they want to be noticed. When they behave in unacceptable ways, ignore them—don't

give them the attention they want. Be sure to give them lots of attention when they're behaving in positive ways.

PRESCHOOLERS

- Help preschoolers learn the skills they need to avoid being bullies or victims. For example, teach them to say, "No, I don't want to do that." If that doesn't work, tell them to walk away and get help from an adult.
- Help preschoolers work through their feelings about a conflict. Ask each child to name his feelings and to understand how the other child might feel. Say, "Can you think of some peaceful ways to solve the problem?" Suggest solutions if children can't come up with any on their own.
- Talk to preschoolers about name calling. Ask, "How does it feel when someone calls you names?" Let preschoolers know that words can be just as hurtful as fists.

RESOURCE

We Can Get Along: A Child's Book of Choices by Lauren Murphy Payne, M.S.W., and Claudia Rohling, M.S.W. (Minneapolis: Free Spirit Publishing, 1997), teaches children ages 3–8 essential conflict-resolution and peacemaking skills. Has a companion leader's guide.

- Break up fights between preschoolers. While it's important for children to learn how to settle disputes on their own, adults have a duty to keep children from hurting each other. Teach preschoolers the basics of negotiation and making up. You might give children some simple phrases they can use, such as, "I think you're right," "Let's talk about this," and "I'm sorry."
- Bullying behavior can start during the preschool years. If you see a child bullying others, let her know right away that you don't approve of her behavior. Teach her peaceful conflict resolution skills now to avoid problems in the future.

DID YOU KNOW?

Bullying is *not* "just part of growing up." Getting teased, picked on, pushed around, threatened, and insulted—or doing these things to others—isn't okay. With the help of caring adults, children can respect each other, support each other, and find positive ways to settle conflicts.

Source: Allan L. Beane, Ph.D., *The Bully Free Classroom* (Minneapolis: Free Spirit Publishing, 1999).

ELEMENTARY-AGE CHILDREN

- Tell children, "Violence is never a good way to solve problems. When you're angry or frustrated, you need to find a peaceful way to share your feelings." Help children come up with a "peace plan" for times when they're upset. For example, if a child has a problem with another child, each person can take a turn talking about the problem and how they feel about it. Together, the children can come up with some solutions. They can talk about how these might work, then choose one. After they've tried it, they can meet again to talk about how the solution worked.

RESOURCE

Sadako Peace Project for Children
P.O. Box 1253
Issaquah, WA 98027-1253
Telephone: (425) 391-4797
Web site: *www.sadako.org/SadakoHome.htm*

This organization links children who want to be pen pals with other children who are interested in world peace.

- Feelings can grow and change over time. For example, irritation can intensify into anger, which may lead to aggressive actions. Teach children to identify and cope with feelings that could create problems later.

- Teach children to use "I-messages" to share their feelings. Instead of saying "YOU make me so mad," have children say "I feel mad." For example: "I feel mad when you make up stories about me that aren't true. Please stop it."

- Children sometimes fight because they don't know how to put their feelings into words. Have children look for more creative, constructive ways to settle their differences. (They might suggest taking turns, drawing straws, or talking to a trusted adult.)

ASSETS IN ACTION
Teaching Skills Through Sports

Asset building is an important part of the program at the Mesa Family YMCA in Arizona. Coaches attend special training sessions about the 40 developmental assets and teach children how to resolve conflicts peacefully and make decisions as well as how to shoot a basket or make a slap shot. Bruce L. Shepherd, a roller hockey coach at the Mesa Family Y, says, "I want to help the kids to work together, play their best, and not blame each other when things go wrong."

MORE IDEAS FOR BUILDING THE SOCIAL COMPETENCIES ASSETS

IDEAS FOR PARENTS

- Work out your disagreements with a child. Be respectful and listen to the child's thoughts and opinions. Give him a chance to think about what he'll do and say.
- Plan family cultural celebrations. Each month, choose a different culture to study. Visit the library to learn more about the culture's history and traditions. Cook food and play games from the culture.
- Give your children plenty of opportunities to make appropriate choices throughout the day. For example, a child can choose if she'll wear blue jeans or black jeans, but she can't choose if she'll go to the doctor or to preschool.
- As a family, make a list of many creative and humorous ways to say "No." Make a game of it to help your child think creatively. Try, "I have to go floss my cat's teeth." "I don't do things like that on days that end in Y." (Don't be surprised if your children use many items from the list in the near future.)
- Invite your children's friends to your home. Give children plenty of time to play together and work on their interpersonal skills.

RESOURCES

The Parent's Handbook and *Parenting Young Children* by Don Dinkmeyer et al. (Circle Pines, MN: American Guidance Service, 1997) present a variety of ideas and skills for encouraging children to make responsible choices, handle feelings appropriately, and solve problems peacefully.

IDEAS FOR CHILDCARE PROVIDERS

- Make a "friendship wall." Hang photos of each child at children's eye level.
- Fill a basket with smiley-face stickers. Tell children, "When you do something nice for someone else, you can take a smiley out of the basket and stick it on the friendship wall." Let children take responsibility for their actions and do this on their own.
- Create a peace place in an area of the room, where the "peace puppy" (a stuffed toy) lives. When children fight, have them go to the peace place and hold the peace puppy. (Other children can watch quietly.) Each child can take a turn holding the puppy and saying what happened, how they felt about it, and what they think should happen now.
- Give children reasonable choices. For example, let them choose whether to build with blocks or play with clay.
- Celebrate a different culture each month through books, music, art, play, and dance. Invite children's families or guests to talk about their cultural traditions.

IDEAS FOR EDUCATORS

- Have children select a special holiday or event to celebrate: they might choose Chinese New Year, Black History Month (February), Juneteenth (June 19), Latin American Month (November), Hanukkah, or Santa Lucia Day (December 13). Help them research the holiday and plan a special event or party.
- Talk with students about the importance of friendship in your life. Share stories about your friends. Tell why your friends mean so much to you.
- Write the word "No" on a blank sheet of posterboard. On the poster, have children write the things they say no to (such as drugs, hitting, yelling, alcohol). On another sheet, write the word "Yes." Have children write the things they say yes to on this poster (like friendship, caring, smiles, and so on). Hang both posters on the classroom wall. Have a class discussion about what children have written. Does everyone say "yes" and "no" to the same things? What other ideas do they have?

- Make a special point of welcoming new students. Before the student arrives, talk to the class about ways to be friendly and helpful. Make a welcome banner and greeting cards. Ask for volunteers to be the student's "buddy"—to show him around, sit with him at lunch, and help him feel like an important part of the class. (Switch buddies every day or so.)
- Try out a peer mediation program to teach children how to resolve conflicts peacefully. Ask other educators to suggest programs that have worked for them in the past.

IDEAS FOR HEALTH-CARE PROFESSIONALS

- Get children involved in making choices about their health. For example, even a toddler can choose which bandage to put on after a shot. A preschooler can decide if she wants to be weighed before or after her height is measured.
- Ask children and their parents about eating, sleeping, and exercise choices. Challenge them to improve.
- When children share their feelings, listen and let them know you understand. Be sensitive, but also be clear about what they can expect.
- Have books and toys from many cultures in your waiting rooms and examination areas.
- Watch how children interact with their parents and siblings. Talk to children about taking turns, listening, and negotiating.

IDEAS FOR CONGREGATIONAL LEADERS

- Have children plan parts of congregational events and activities. For example, children can decide what games to play at a congregational potluck.
- Teach children peacemaking skills. Show them how to resolve conflicts in a healthy way, and how to make and keep friends.
- Talk about the connection between resistance skills and positive values. Ask, "How do your values help you decide what to do or what not to do?"

- Celebrate the diversity of your congregation and the world. Have a special religious service that focuses on diversity. Invite children to participate.
- In religious education classes, teach children your faith tradition's stories about peace and reconciliation.

IDEAS FOR EMPLOYERS

- Do children visit your workplace? If so, give them a chance to make choices. For example, let them choose a special trinket to take home with them.
- When you're planning an event for employees and their families, create a committee of children to help. Let the children plan activities they'll enjoy.
- Put together a list of local help lines, shelters, and other organizations that support families. Distribute this list to employees.
- Support scout groups, boys and girls clubs, after-school programs, and other organizations that help children improve their social skills.

IDEAS FOR LIBRARIANS

- Talk to families about setting book check-out guidelines to help teach children about responsibility and making decisions. For example, some families allow children to check out a number of books equal to their age.
- Hold cooking classes at your library. Invite a local cook to lead sessions about food from many cultures. The cook might also recommend multicultural cookbooks and suggest new dishes that children might enjoy.
- Develop a "book buddy" program where children read books out loud to each other. Children can keep track of the books they read together.
- Create word searches, crossword puzzles, and other fun handouts for children to do when they visit the library. Include words from the social competencies assets, like "peace," "plan," and "decide."

- Highlight heroes (such as Martin Luther King Jr., Aung San Suu Kyi, Dalai Lama, Harriet Tubman, and Mahatma Gandhi) who have promoted nonviolence. Fill a display case with books about them and their ideas.

IDEAS FOR COMMUNITY LEADERS

- Celebrate the diversity of your community by holding heritage festivals. You might have a Cinco de Mayo fiesta in May and an Oktoberfest celebration in October. Include activities for children as part of the event.
- Give children a chance to make their voices heard. Have a group of children identify an improvement they'd like to make in your community's services for children. You can help them make a plan and put it into action.
- Take a look at your children's programs (such as scouting, swimming lessons, and sports). Are these programs accessible to children from all cultural and economic backgrounds? If not, recruit new members or offer scholarships to boost enrollment.
- Offer classes and workshops about each of the social competencies assets. Schedule one set of classes for parents and another for children.

We encourage you to photocopy this page (set the image size at 125 percent), cut out the "Ideas for Children," and share them with a child you know.

IDEAS FOR CHILDREN:
BUILD YOUR OWN SOCIAL COMPETENCIES ASSETS

- Practice making decisions and plans. If things don't turn out as you expected, find out why. How can you change your plan and make it better?

- What do *you* like to do? Make a plan to do something special, then put your plan into action.

- Practice saying "Yes" and "No." Don't be afraid to use these words when you need them.

- Use words to let people know how you feel. Talking about things that bother you can help you feel better sometimes.

- Find peaceful ways to solve a conflict. For example, talk respectfully about how you feel instead of fighting or yelling. If a problem's hard to solve, talk about it with an adult you trust.

- People come in all colors, shapes, and sizes, with different thoughts and ideas. Read books that tell you what life is like for other people.

- Imagine that you could travel anywhere in the world. Where would you go? Learn more about that place and the people who live there.

THE POSITIVE
IDENTITY ASSETS

Caring adults can sow the seeds of positive identity as soon as a child enters the world. While children grow, their sense of self needs to be cultivated and nurtured so they can learn who they are and what they can do. Adults around them can challenge, support, and guide children as they move through childhood and are on their way to becoming confident adolescents and adults.

The positive identity category includes four developmental assets for children from birth through age 11:

The Positive Identity Assets

Asset 37: Personal Power

Asset 38: Self-Esteem

Asset 39: Sense of Purpose

Asset 40: Positive View of Personal Future

When Search Institute surveyed 6th graders, they found that children experience some of the positive identity assets more than others. Here are the percentages of these children who reported each of the assets in their lives:

Asset 37: Personal Power	**40%**
Asset 38: Self-Esteem	**52%**
Asset 39: Sense of Purpose	**57%**
Asset 40: Positive View of Personal Future	**72%**

Asset 37

PERSONAL POWER

Parents and other adults model coping skills, demonstrating healthy ways to deal with frustrations and challenges. Children learn that they can influence their surroundings and have control over things that happen to them.

How Search Institute defines this asset . . .

For infants, toddlers, and preschoolers: Parents feel they have control over things that happen in their own lives and model coping skills, demonstrating healthy ways to deal with frustrations and challenges. Parents respond to children so children begin to learn that they have influence over their immediate surroundings.

For elementary-age children: Children begin to feel they have control over things that happen to them. They begin to manage frustrations and challenges in ways that have positive results for themselves and others.

ALL CHILDREN

- Let children play and do things their own way sometimes. If they enjoy looking at books backwards and upside down, or want to wash and dry each dish one at a time, don't interfere.
- Children have many different interests and talents. Encouraging them to follow their interests can give them a sense of power.

- Create boundaries that help children build their own sense of self-control or mastery rather than just follow the commands of adults. Make rules ahead of time so children can begin to work within them. For example, when children know they are to finish their homework before playing, they can decide which homework to complete first and which to do last.

INFANTS

- Respond to infants' needs in consistent ways. Babies tell you what they need by crying, fussing, or turning their head away. If they let you know they're hungry, feed them; if they let you know they're wet, change them. This begins to teach them that they can influence the world around them.

- Infants like to drop things to watch them fall. Make this a fun game. After an infant drops something, give it back to him so he'll drop it again.

- Give an infant toys that rattle or make different sounds when she plays with them. Making something happen builds an infant's sense of personal power.

- When infants are ready for solid food, begin to give them finger foods that they can eat by themselves.

 DID YOU KNOW?

Children begin to develop a sense of personal power—or the lack of it—at a very young age. When they're born, children can only control the muscles they use for eye movements and for sucking. Over the next few months, infants slowly learn to control their arms and legs. Flailing arms become reaching arms. Children then learn to crawl, walk, and talk. Children's control over themselves grows at each of these important milestones.

Source: Martin E.P. Seligman, *The Optimistic Child* (Boston: Houghton Mifflin, 1995).

- Mimic an infant's actions. For example, if a baby bangs his hands on the table, bang your hands on the table in the same way. When you follow his lead, he gains a sense of power.
- Slowly introduce infants to new experiences. Watch how they respond, so you know when they're ready for more.

TODDLERS

- Toddlers say "No" as part of developing a sense of independence. Be patient and positive with them.
- When toddlers say things like "Me do it," let them. Give them plenty of time and space to work on their skills. (Make sure that what they want to do is safe and appropriate.)
- Many toddlers have a special blanket or a favorite stuffed animal. Respect the importance of these items; they're comforting when a toddler feels stressed or tired.
- Let a toddler decide what to play sometimes. Follow her lead.
- Give toddlers plenty of time to play by themselves. This helps them learn more about their interests and become more self-reliant. Be responsive to their cues that they've had enough.
- Reassure a toddler who cries or clings. Give him lots of comfort and attention. When a toddler feels secure, he's more willing to explore on his own.

PRESCHOOLERS

- Give children the freedom to play and experiment with different toys. Their sense of personal power grows when they can make choices.
- Allow preschoolers to do the things they think are fun. If a preschooler likes taking her shoes off and putting them on again, let her do this.
- Many movie companies publish a movie storybook before releasing a children's film. Read the book together before you rent a movie or go to the theater. Talk about anything that might scare the preschooler. (Trust your instincts. If you think the movie may frighten the child, don't go.) Knowing the story in advance gives a preschooler a sense of control and power.

- Help preschoolers learn new skills. For example, hold your hand on a preschooler's tricycle the first time he rides down a small hill. Then move to walking alongside the preschooler until he's comfortable with his abilities.
- Take tiny steps to help preschoolers overcome their fears. For example, if a child is afraid of dogs, share a book with pictures of dogs. Talk about what dogs are like. Be patient and wait until the child is ready to make friends with a dog.

ELEMENTARY-AGE CHILDREN

- Respect the decisions a child makes. If you don't agree, talk honestly with the child about your concerns. Having choices respected gives children a sense of control over their lives.
- Children can control what they say and do, but they can't control what other people say and do. Help children understand and accept this. For example, you might explain, "You can't make Kelly come play if she doesn't want to. But you can decide what you'll do to feel better about it."
- Read about children and adults who overcame difficult situations. Say, "People can do great things when they set their mind to it." Talk together about what you learn.
- Ask children about their dreams and passions. What are they doing to reach them? Give children the space they need to follow their dreams, but also take steps to support them. For example, a child who loves trains can play with a train set alone, but needs an adult to take her to a train station to ride a train.

RESOURCE

Stick Up for Yourself! Every Kid's Guide to Personal Power and Positive Self-Esteem by Gershen Kaufman, Ph.D., Lev Rafael, Ph.D., and Pamela Espeland (Minneapolis: Free Spirit Publishing, 1999) includes strategies for building personal power, assertiveness skills, and self-esteem. For ages 8 to 12. A teacher's guide is also available.

- Find ways for children to feel proud of their accomplishments. Scout badges or 4-H ribbons are a great way to help build a child's personal power.
- Talk about the characters you see on television. Who is a powerful person? Who isn't? Who just acts powerful?

ASSETS IN ACTION
Making a Better Future

When the library and other parts of Colorado State University (CSU) in Fort Collins were damaged by a flash flood, 9-year-old Amanda Wallace believed that college students could use some hope—and some help. She organized a read-a-thon called "Pennies for Pages." She asked area families to pay children a penny for every page they read for 30 days. She set a goal of earning $300. She reached that goal, and went beyond it. The children brought in 72,516 pennies, and a very happy Wallace delivered a check for $725.16 to the CSU library.

Asset 38

SELF-ESTEEM

Parents and other adults model high self-esteem and give children appropriate positive feedback. Children learn to feel good about themselves.

How Search Institute defines this asset . . .

For infants, toddlers, and preschoolers: Parents create an environment where children can develop positive self-esteem, giving children appropriate, positive feedback and reinforcement about their skills and competencies.

For elementary-age children: Children report having high self-esteem.

ALL CHILDREN

- People with a strong sense of self-esteem take care of themselves. Model this for children.
- Accept and appreciate children as individuals. Be patient and support children as they learn and grow at their own rate.
- Do things *with* children, not just *for* them. Although children love getting presents, the best gift you can give them is your time and attention. This shows them that they're important to you.
- Show your concern for children by what you do as well as what you say. For example, make eye contact with children

when you talk to them. Smile. Give them your full attention and let them know you care.

RESOURCE

The Winning Family by Louise Hart (Berkeley, CA: Celestial Arts, 1996) suggests how parents can increase self-esteem in their children and themselves.

INFANTS

- Love infants unconditionally. Hold them and cuddle them. This teaches them that they're special and valuable, and that you enjoy being with them.
- Protect and care for infants. A safe and secure environment gives infants the support they need to develop self-esteem.
- Do whatever you can to meet an infant's needs. Show him how important he is.
- Model self-respect for infants. It's never too early for children to be around adults who think well of themselves. This will eventually help children think well of themselves, too.
- Choose an infant's name carefully. When the child is older, talk about the child's name and why you chose it. Help the child feel proud of her name.

TODDLERS

- What can you do to help toddlers succeed? You might place step stools in front of sinks and light switches so toddlers can wash their hands and turn lights on and off by themselves. Toddlers feel good about themselves when they can do things on their own.
- When a toddler is frustrated, offer plenty of encouragement and support. But be sure the child has a chance to try new things and develop new skills independently, too.

- Celebrate toddlers' originality and enthusiasm. Dance with them to music. Play the games they create. Do what they want to do.
- Give toddlers lots of individual attention. This teaches them that they're worthwhile.
- Some toddlers love playing with sand. Others enjoy building cities with blocks. Whatever they like, make sure they have a chance to do it often.

PRESCHOOLERS

- Help preschoolers feel good about themselves and their accomplishments. Give them a bulletin board where they can hang their artwork. Carry a camera with you and take pictures of the preschooler doing new things. Tell friends and family about preschoolers' adventures and the things they've learned.
- An enhancing environment helps preschoolers improve their skills, follow their interests, and build their self-esteem. For example, make sure an art-loving child has lots of markers, paints, crayons, and paper available.

 DID YOU KNOW?

"Self-esteem is shaped and reshaped as we interact with each other and our environment," write Nancy E. Curry and Carl N. Johnson. Infants and toddlers are just starting to learn about themselves. Preschoolers are further expanding, testing, and evaluating themselves. In elementary school, children begin to measure themselves against new standards. Love, acceptance, and support are building blocks for a child's self-esteem.

Source: Nancy E. Curry and Carl N. Johnson, *Beyond Self-Esteem: Developing a Genuine Sense of Human Value* (Washington, DC: National Association for the Education of Young Children, 1990).

- Show preschoolers that what they do is important to you. Go to programs at their preschools. When they show you things, be attentive and ask questions.
- Create projects and tasks that help preschoolers learn about themselves. You might say, "Let's go to the library. You can pick some books that look interesting."
- Give a preschooler your undivided attention for some period of time every day. Let the preschooler decide how to spend the time together.
- Be caring and supportive when preschoolers have had a tough day. Help them find appropriate ways to express their feelings—no matter what those feelings are.

ELEMENTARY-AGE CHILDREN

- What do children like to do? Find out. Show you care by asking questions and then sharing their interests.
- Recognize children when they do things well. Tell them what you think to let them know you noticed. For example, say, "Great catch!" or "What a neat ending to your story."
- Some children are sensitive about their appearance, especially if they feel different from people around them. Talk to children about their thoughts and feelings on a variety of issues. Let children know that no two people are alike and that this makes our world interesting.
- Have children create an "All About Me Book." In a blank notebook or scrapbook, ask children to write about their families, their favorite school subject, their proudest moment, their biggest dream, and so on. Have children paste in photographs or drawings and special mementos of events (such as school programs or newspaper articles). Children can choose to share their books or keep them to themselves.
- When children act inappropriately, focus on the *behavior*, not on the child. Remember that a child's self-esteem can be fragile. Handle it with care and love. Don't say, "You're so irresponsible!" Instead, say, "That wasn't a responsible thing to do. Let's talk about it."

Asset 39

SENSE OF PURPOSE

Parents and other adults feel and show that their lives have purpose. Children are curious and interested in exploring the world around them. As children grow, they feel that their life has purpose.

How Search Institute defines this asset . . .

For infants: Parents report that their lives have purpose and demonstrate these beliefs through their behaviors. Infants are curious about the world around them.

For toddlers and preschoolers: Parents report that their lives have purpose and model these beliefs through their behaviors. Children are curious and explore the world around them.

For elementary-age children: Children report that their lives have purpose and actively engage their skills.

ALL CHILDREN

- Be in touch with what's important to you. Share this with the children in your life. You might say, "I walk every day to stay healthy. Walking makes me feel great. And I keep working at it because someday I want to be able to take a hiking trip through the mountains."

- Examine your list of dreams and goals. What have you always wanted to do that you haven't tried yet? Taking voice lessons or studying another language (if that's something you've always wanted to do) tells children that you believe it's important to follow your interests.
- Inspire hope by being hopeful, interest by being interested. Let children see that you're enthusiastic about life; talk about your feelings with children.

INFANTS

- Infants are naturally curious. Let them learn and try new things. For example, if a 7-month-old is determined to crawl across the room to get a ball, get out of the way and let him do what he wants to do in a safe environment.
- Find ways for infants to be around people who enjoy what they do. Let them enjoy the charged atmosphere where people are following their dreams.
- Parents of an infant have a special purpose—to care for their baby. This means that they're always available and that they meet an infant's need right away.
- Let older infants choose what they want to play with. Give them as much time as they need to explore the toy they pick. As they learn what interests them, they take the first steps toward developing a sense of purpose.

TODDLERS

- Make a toddler's life interesting and stimulating. For a toddler, a meaningful day includes many different activities and experiences—music, art projects, quiet time, outdoor games, and so on.
- Pay attention to what toddlers enjoy. Respect their likes and dislikes. Any toy or activity that holds a toddler's attention for a long time helps build a sense of purpose.
- Find a way to include a toddler in activities you enjoy. For example, if you love to run, take a toddler to the track with you and let her run on her own in a safe area.

- Listen when a toddler says, "Again! Again!" Toddlers learn by repetition. Let them do the things they like to do.

PRESCHOOLERS

- Preschoolers have some activities they especially enjoy, but continue to give them many choices of things to do. Something yet undiscovered may someday become a favorite.
- Preschoolers are curious and ask lots of questions about things that interest them. Give them honest answers.
- Playing dress-up (in preschool this is often called dramatic play) is a fun way for preschoolers to try out different roles. Ask children what they like about being a doctor, firefighter, or clown.
- When preschoolers are fascinated by a certain idea or activity, they're learning and developing their interests. Don't worry if they seem single-minded. When they're ready, they'll move on to something else.

ELEMENTARY-AGE CHILDREN

- Create an atmosphere where children feel free to discover. Ask questions. "What do you like to do at school? at home? What makes you want to jump out of bed in the morning?"
- Go out of your way to help children follow their passions. For example, take a child who loves trains to the train station. Arrange a tour of the engine and the train cars.
- Collect inspiring quotations. Hang them on bathroom mirrors, doors, refrigerators, and hallway walls. Have children collect and post their favorite sayings, too.
- Teach children that chasing their dreams isn't always easy. It's normal to get discouraged and want to quit once in a while. Support children while they get their second wind and rediscover their interest.
- Ask children to list the things they enjoy doing. Then have them rank these activities. How can they find more ways to do the top things on their list?

- Have a child interview an adult role model (such as a relative or neighbor) to learn more about what gives purpose to the person's life. The child might ask, "What do you like to do? How long have you been excited about this? When did you discover that you enjoyed or wanted to do it? What do you like about it most? What advice do you have for people who haven't discovered what they like yet?"

RESOURCE

Kids Cheering Kids
P.O. Box 2359
Las Gatos, CA 95031
Toll-free phone: 1-888-KIDS PLAY (1-888-543-7752)
Web site: *www.kidscheeringkids.org*

This organization helps people from ages 5 to 23 come together with a sense of purpose to create a better world for all children. Members share their time, ideas, money, and optimism.

Asset 40

POSITIVE VIEW OF PERSONAL FUTURE

Parents and other adults work to create a positive future for themselves and their children. As children mature, they are hopeful and positive about their future.

How Search Institute defines this asset . . .

For infants, toddlers, and preschoolers: Parents are hopeful and positive about their personal future and work to provide a positive future for children.

For elementary-age children: Children are hopeful and positive about their personal future.

ALL CHILDREN

- Expect good things to happen. When disappointments come along, see them as unusual events. Children learn how to handle setbacks and challenges by watching the adults around them.
- Give children plenty of sincere, positive feedback. When you share good words with them, you help them feel successful. Limit your negative comments as much as you can.
- Find ways for children to follow their dreams and passions. Share in their excitement. For example, if a child loves music, fill the home with it. Ask the child to teach you songs, sing

along with the radio together, plan musical events, and look for a way to provide music lessons.

- There are some children who seem to have a temperament that often makes them see things negatively or pessimistically. Teach these children lots of positive ways to think about the world. For example, if a child feels frustrated or overwhelmed, have him think about something else he's accomplished. Say, "If you can do that, think about what else you might do!"
- Examine your own outlook on life. Read a book like *Learned Optimism* by Martin E.P. Seligman, Ph.D. (New York: Pocket Books, 1998), which includes tools to rate yourself and practical ways to increase your own optimism.

RESOURCE

The Optimistic Child by Martin E.P. Seligman, Ph.D. (Boston: Houghton Mifflin, 1995), gives step-by-step advice on how to safeguard children from depression while helping them develop optimism and a positive view of the future.

INFANTS

- Nurture babies with unconditional love and care. This helps them see that the world is a positive place.
- Respond to infants in caring ways. For example, when infants smile, smile back at them. When they cry, rub them gently and speak reassuringly.
- Let infants see that their actions matter. For example, show babies how to make a special stuffed toy sing a song. They'll learn that they can influence the world around them.
- Meet an infant's needs immediately. The importance of doing this can't be stressed enough. It not only helps the infant now, but teaches her that you'll take care of her in the future.

TODDLERS

- Use small steps to introduce toddlers to new challenges. This will help them complete tasks without feeling frustrated and look forward to what comes next.
- Increase a toddler's play space as he grows. Build on the skills he already has and give him a chance to explore.
- Let toddlers make choices. (For more on this, see Asset 32: Planning and Decision Making, pages 231–235.) Get them involved in making decisions about their future. Start small: ask, "What things do you want to do when you grow up?"

PRESCHOOLERS

- What are preschoolers watching on television? Talk about the characters (especially the heroes) who are optimistic.
- Have preschoolers use dolls or stuffed animals to act out frustrating experiences. Be available to ask questions and suggest positive ways to solve the problem.
- Use only positive and encouraging phrases around preschoolers. For example, say, "Let's try it" instead of "That won't work" or "That looks hard" when you face a difficult situation. Have a preschooler repeat, "I'll find a way to make this work." Then brainstorm some possible solutions together.
- Plan fun with preschoolers. It's hard to be negative about the present—and the future—when you're having a good time.

ELEMENTARY-AGE CHILDREN

- Practice being positive. When children assume bad things will happen, talk about different ways the situation could work out favorably.
- When children behave appropriately, reward them. Thank them. It can be all too easy to focus on what kids do wrong. Let them know when they do something right.
- Teach children how to identify their feelings and use specific words to describe them. For example, a young goalie who lets the winning shot get past her may say, "I hate myself." You

might respond, "You're upset about not blocking that goal. You sound frustrated with yourself."

- Between the ages of 7 and 10, many children struggle with their self-image. They may compare themselves to others and feel that they don't measure up. Don't dismiss children's uncomfortable feelings, but help them see the big picture. Let them know they're valuable and special.

 DID YOU KNOW?

Researchers have learned that young people who feel that they don't have a future may be at risk for emotional and behavioral problems. When kids face conflicts in their families, physical punishment, and violence, they're more likely to feel hopeless.

Source: R.H. DuRant et al., "Exposure to Violence and Victimization and Depression, Hopelessness, and Purpose in Life Among Adolescents Living in and around Public Housing." *Journal of Developmental and Behavioral Pediatrics* 16 (1995).

MORE IDEAS FOR BUILDING THE POSITIVE IDENTITY ASSETS

IDEAS FOR PARENTS

- Show your love and support for your children throughout the year. Give children valentine cards and candy hearts often, at any time of year, to let them know how you feel about them.
- Notice what your children enjoy doing. Be enthusiastic about their passions. Find opportunities to make their dreams come true. For example, see if a child who loves horses can help care for the animals at a stable.
- Start a special birthday tradition. After the birthday person blows out the candles on the cake, give each birthday guest a piece of cake with a candle on it. (You may need to have extra candles for this.) Light each candle. Let everyone take turns making a wish for the birthday person, then blow out their candle.

ASSETS IN ACTION
"I Did That!"

After the birth of a baby girl, the father of a 2-year-old boy thought of a way his son could build assets—he asked the 2-year-old to teach his baby sister how to smile. Before long the sister began responding to her brother with a pleasant expression. When she grinned back at him for the first time, he proudly announced, "I did that!" The interaction between the two children helped to stave off jealousy and to build a bond between the two. Even better, it helped the 2-year-old develop a sense of personal power and improve his self-esteem.

- Children may act immaturely when they're stressed, overtired, sick, or experiencing a major change (such as when a sibling joins the family). This kind of behavior is generally temporary, but lets you know that you need to give the child lots of extra love and support.
- Create a family hall of fame in one of your home's hallways. Hang up art projects, photographs, outstanding assignments, awards, and anything else. Make sure everyone in the family adds something to the display.

IDEAS FOR CHILDCARE PROVIDERS

- Spend time on the floor with children. Hold them. Hug them. Pat their backs. Caring for children will help them form a positive identity.
- Make your childcare center a gallery of children's art. Take children on "tours" of the gallery. Have them point out their work and say, "I did that!"
- Include sharing time in your daily or weekly schedule. Gather children in a circle and ask them to tell a little bit about themselves. Choose specific topics, such as "My favorite animal," "What I like about spring (or another season)," or "What I want to be when I grow up."
- Tell children when you see them behaving appropriately. "I like it when you help pick up the toys." "That was nice of you to give Hannah a hug when she was crying."
- Start a "Star of the Week" or "Big Cheese" bulletin board. Each week, have a different child bring in pictures of himself to decorate the board. Create a special crown (a star or a piece of "cheese") for the honored child to wear during the week.
- Expect children to reach developmental milestones at their own pace. Don't push them or compare them to others. Applaud them as they make progress.

IDEAS FOR EDUCATORS

- Create a classroom newspaper featuring students' stories, poems, and artwork. Publish a special edition at the start of each year that shares a little bit about each child in the class.

- Ask students to bring in clean, light-colored T-shirts from home (have extra shirts on hand for children whose families don't send one). Provide nontoxic fabric paints and fabric markers. Have children draw or write words on the shirts that describe themselves.

- Talk about the difference between pessimistic and optimistic language. Teach children how to correct negative talk and use positive statements instead.

- Ask, "What is it like to have power? What is it like not to have power?" Have students discuss what they can do when they feel powerless.

- Give helpful feedback when critiquing assignments and tests. Write, "I like this" or "How creative!" Suggest ways a student can improve: "Can you make this sound as lively as the first paragraph?" "You seemed to understand all the questions on the first page. What do you think stopped you here?"

- Create a classroom caring corner. Fill the space with pillows and stuffed animals, and hang encouraging posters on the walls. If a student is having a tough day, the child can sit in the space for a few minutes to rest and think.

IDEAS FOR HEALTH-CARE PROFESSIONALS

- Write down things you learn about patients. For example, if you discover that a patient loves playing soccer, make a note in her file. Next time you see her, ask her something like, "How are you enjoying soccer this year?" This lets children know that you care about them as people, not just as patients.

- Be a leader. Speak out about ways your community can promote the health and well-being of children.

- Display photos of the children who visit your facilities. Some hospitals even post a picture of each newborn.

- Ask children what their dreams are. Be interested. Help them find ways to develop their dreams even more. For example, if a child loves dinosaurs, show her a book on dinosaurs that you keep in the children's waiting area, or tell her and her family about a dinosaur exhibit at a local museum.

- A sick child may feel hopeless and pessimistic. Be hopeful and optimistic. Respect the child's feelings, but show you care and want to help him feel better.
- Let young patients know what you like about them. You might say, "You ask really good questions" or "You have a great positive attitude." Tell them how much you appreciate them.

IDEAS FOR CONGREGATIONAL LEADERS

- How does your congregation make decisions? Find a way to include children's perspectives. Listen to their ideas. Put their suggestions into practice.
- Make a helping hands display for everyone in your congregation to see. Have all the children in your congregation trace their hands on a piece of paper. Cut out the hands and have children write their names on them, along with activities they enjoy and words that describe them. Hang the paper hands in a prominent place.
- Find out the birthdays and adoption arrival dates of all the children in your congregation. Mention these special days in religious service bulletins and your congregational newsletter.
- Religious education classes can do special activities to improve children's positive identity. For example, a class could work on building self-esteem by having children say positive, caring things to each other.
- In your religious service bulletin, share a story about a different child each week. Ask the child to give a reading, carry a candle, or participate in another way in a service that week. Thank the child for being a part of your congregation.
- Study people who are important to your faith tradition. Choose a current leader and someone from your faith's history. Have children learn more about these people's hopes and dreams. What did they do to make their dreams come true?

IDEAS FOR EMPLOYERS

- How can your organization bring out the best in children? Create a task force or committee to find out.

- Have an annual toy swap. On this day, employees can bring in gently used toys, children's clothing, and other children's items to exchange.
- If your company provides grants or contributes money to organizations, have children help you decide where the money goes.
- Distribute the list of 40 developmental assets to employees. Give them the lists that fit the ages of their children. (You'll find lists for photocopying on pages 14–23.)
- Go out of your way to talk with children who visit your workplace.

IDEAS FOR LIBRARIANS

- Create a banner that says "What I Like About Me." Have children who visit the library write their name and something they like about themselves on the banner. Hang the banner in a place of honor.
- Make cozy reading havens for children in your library. For example, one library made a large catcher's mitt for children to sit in.
- Have a storytelling workshop where children share stories about themselves with each other. (Develop a list of story-starters, like "The best day I ever had was . . . " or "My favorite place is . . . " to help children who can't think of what to say.) Record the children's stories on tapes or CDs.
- Put together a list of books that can help children get to know themselves better. Make copies of the list for children to take with them.
- Celebrate Dream Day on August 28. Create a display around Martin Luther King Jr.'s famous "I Have a Dream" speech. Encourage children to write or draw pictures of their own dreams. Post the results around the library.

IDEAS FOR COMMUNITY LEADERS

- Get your community to make the concerns of children and youth a top priority. Some communities have created asset-building initiatives with an emphasis on children, such as

Kids at Las Sendas in Mesa, Arizona; Children First in St. Louis Park, Minnesota; What Kids Need to Succeed in Boulder County, Colorado; and It's About Time . . . For Kids in Seattle, Washington. These initiatives create opportunities and programs to build children's assets through many sectors of the community, including schools, congregations, children's clubs, neighborhoods, health-care systems, childcare centers, libraries, and businesses.

- Offer activities for children that develop and strengthen their self-esteem. For example, teach them things they can grasp quickly (like how to make simple origami animals).

- Include children in programs that celebrate your community. In Vinalhaven, an island community in the gulf of Maine, organizers of a community celebration asked people of various age groups (both children and adults) to talk about what they thought was good about their community.

- Highlight children who have contributed to community life in significant ways. Invite them to meet the mayor or city council and have their picture taken. Ask the local newspaper to write an article about each child you recognize.

- Recognize organizations and individuals who are making a difference in the lives of children. For example, a grocery store may designate special parking spots for pregnant women and families with young children. This good deed might inspire other businesses to do the same.

- Let children plan and do projects like creating a community garden or cleaning up a playground.

We encourage you to photocopy this page (set the image size at 125 percent), cut out the "Ideas for Children," and share them with a child you know.

IDEAS FOR CHILDREN:
BUILDING YOUR OWN POSITIVE IDENTITY ASSETS

- Challenge yourself by trying new things. You don't know what will happen until you try!

- Everyone gets frustrated sometimes. When this happens to you, slow down. Take a break and think through your plan.

- What are your dreams? What do you look forward to? Make a plan for your future. Talk to friends or adults who are interested in helping you make your dreams come true.

- Remember that you're a special person. Feel good about who you are and what you can do.

- Spend time with people who help you feel good about yourself. Find friends who care about you and help you do your best.

MAKING ASSET BUILDING
PART OF YOUR EVERYDAY LIFE

Making asset building part of your everyday life is easy. It doesn't take a lot of time or money. You don't have to have experience. All you need is the belief that children are important and that people need to be there to support them, guide them, and cheer them on. Building assets in children helps you bring out the best in them—and in you.

STEPS TO BUILDING CHILDREN'S ASSETS

You can begin building children's assets in three simple steps:

1. **Believe that children deserve your attention and care.** If you believe this, you've taken the first step.

2. **Make a commitment.** What small, simple things can you do to build assets? Go easy on yourself. You don't need to sign up to be a soccer coach or become a scout leader if you don't want to. Start with something like smiling at every child you see during your day.

3. **Act.** Do what you set out to do. Learn the names of the children who live in your neighborhood and go out of your way to say hello to them. Jump rope with them. Applaud when they do somersaults and cartwheels. Laugh at their knock-knock jokes and make up silly rhymes with them. Find the child within you and let that child come out to play.

Getting Started

You can do small, simple acts of asset building for a long time. These little things *do* make a difference. For example, you may discover that children whose names you've learned are going out of their way to say hello to *you*. Asset building isn't only about giving (although it may feel that way when you start). Asset building is also about developing relationships and becoming an important part of your neighborhood or community.

You can go deeper with assets, too. You may be inspired to find new ways to enhance children's lives. Besides building individual assets, you might become a children's advocate. Making the world a better place for children is an important part of asset building.

The ABCs and XYZs of Asset Building

Asset building can be as simple or complex as you'd like. It can use a little of your time, or a lot of it. It all depends on what you want to do. Many people prefer to start small. If this is true for you, follow the ABCs of asset building and do easy, quick things to build assets in children. If you want to have a greater impact, use the XYZs of asset building as a guide to building assets in deeper, long-term ways.

Building assets can take only a few minutes of your time—or years of your life, depending on what you choose to do. You can choose to build assets in three major ways: as an individual, as part of an organization, or as part of a community. It doesn't matter which way (or ways) you choose. All that matters is that you *start*.

ABCs of Asset Building	XYZs of Asset Building
• Quick	• Slower
• Offer immediate results	• Lead to long-term results
• Don't take long	• Take more time
• Need little preparation	• Require preparation
• Simple	• More complex
• Spontaneous	• Intentional
• Easy commitment	• Greater commitment
• Require little energy	• Require more energy

BUILDING ASSETS AS AN INDIVIDUAL

Most people start building assets on their own, as individuals. Researchers agree that one caring adult can change the life of a child. This doesn't mean you have to devote your entire life to a child. Small acts of caring and reaching out often mean more to a child than we can imagine. One adult who had a difficult childhood says, "I've wondered for a long time how to thank the adults who were silver threads of hope for me, the ones who provided a connection to the real world, who gave me something to strive for."

Who were the silver threads of hope in your life? Most of us can name a teacher, a neighbor, a grandparent, a coach—an adult who may not have spent a lot of time with us but who gave enough to make an imprint on our lives. Individuals *do* make a difference. Consider these examples:

- One father posted the list of the 40 developmental assets on the refrigerator and started taking an asset-building approach to parenting. He began to focus on what his kids were doing *right* instead of pointing out what they were doing *wrong*.

- Jill Terry, affectionately known as the "Bus Stop Lady," has been supervising the bus stops in her St. Louis Park, Minnesota, neighborhood for more than nine years. Originally she did this as a way to help keep children safe, but she and the students began to form a bond. She's now the person kids call when they forget their lunch money or need someone to talk to. She even sets and enforces boundaries at the bus stops she frequents. When one child objected to her rules and said, "Mind your own business," Jill told him, "You *are* my business."

- Linda Kemper thought asset building was a great idea, but her only child was grown and lived away from home. She looked around the neighborhood and noticed some of the kids passing a basketball in the street. So she bought a basketball hoop and put it up in her driveway. She told the neighborhood children that they could use the hoop whenever they wanted. They could come over when she was home and when she was away. It's her driveway, but the neighborhood's basketball hoop.

- Teenagers in Glenwood Springs, Colorado, created an asset-building coloring book, which the *Glenwood Post* printed on newsprint. The coloring book was given to children in the community. Other children in the town baked fortune cookies with asset-building messages inside. The children sold the cookies to raise money for projects to help them build assets.

- A teenager in Albuquerque, New Mexico, created an asset-building comic book. Children and teenagers in the community learned more about building assets in a fun way.

- When Georgetown, Texas, created an asset-building initiative, community leaders asked people to create and submit their own logo designs. The winner was 11-year-old Casey Callaham of Pickett Elementary School. She drew two hands coming together to form a heart. Inside the heart are two children, a boy and a girl.

- Fred Getty was dismayed to realize that his adopted children had to wait 30 days for health insurance, while children who were born to their parents were accepted for insurance immediately. For advice, he turned to his state representative, who suggested that Fred might have the basis for a new bill. So Fred researched the facts, advocated for the bill, and lobbied all the legislators in his state. Five years later, the bill was passed. His children already had their insurance coverage by then, but for Fred Getty, this was a step in the right direction to help all children.

BUILDING ASSETS AS AN ORGANIZATION

Organizations have a unique role in building assets in children. Not only can they help by supporting employees who build assets on their own, but they can also develop asset-building strategies that improve the whole community, as in these situations:

- A school involved in the "Ozarks Fighting Back" initiative in Springfield, Missouri, printed the community's asset-building logo on report-card envelopes. To spread the word about asset building, the initiative also created building blocks with assets written on each side.

- In St. Louis Park, Minnesota, the school district raised awareness about asset building through its school calendar. Each month of the calendar featured a specific asset category and gave ideas on ways to build those assets. Since then, the school district has published calendars with art created by children in elementary school, middle school, and high school. The schools within the district made asset building the focus for a whole school year and made asset building a part of the curriculum. The schools' teachers have been trained in asset building. The list of 40 assets is posted in classrooms and in hallways, and published in the school newspaper that goes home to parents each month.

- The community's asset-building logo is painted on school buses for the Cherry Creek School District in Englewood, Colorado. At the district's Belleview Elementary School, the Parent Teacher Organization (PTO) made asset building a part of its goals and objectives, and the school newspaper includes a monthly column where children share stories about building assets.

- As part of an annual fund-raiser at Mercy Medical Center in Nampa, Idaho, one lucky child always won a bicycle. To help build the self-esteem of many children instead of just one, the hospital decided to try something different one year. Instead of a bike giveaway, a vintage convertible made a special appearance. The back of the convertible was filled with balls of many different kinds—soccer balls, tennis balls, basketballs— which were given out to all the children. Every child present felt special and supported.

- Bethlehem Lutheran Church in Minneapolis, Minnesota, offers a "Parent's Day Out" every December. Members of the congregation's junior and senior high youth group provide childcare and activities for children from 6 months to 6th grade. They help the children bake cookies and make cards for homebound church members. Then the preschoolers and younger elementary children deliver the cookies and cards while singing carols. Adults and older teenagers take the 4th, 5th, and 6th graders shopping to buy toys for children who otherwise wouldn't get any toys for the holidays. (The money comes from a 4th-grade fund-raiser.)

- ASAP, a network of 30 community organizations on the north side of Chicago, teamed up with Weiss Memorial Hospital to provide a tutoring program for children from area public housing buildings. Twenty hospital volunteers, including three physicians, helped children individually with their homework. They also gave children insight about careers in health care. Several of the volunteers made a long-term commitment to the children, staying in touch with them during the summer and tutoring them again the following school year.

BUILDING ASSETS AS A COMMUNITY

The assets can help connect residents and organizations in many communities. Some communities have a group of volunteers who brainstorm ways citizens can build assets. Others hire a coordinator to run a complex asset-building initiative. Any approach is fine, as long as it brings residents together to support and empower children, as in these examples:

- A network of 11 asset-building communities in the western suburbs of Minneapolis, Minnesota, holds an annual "We Love Our Kids!" celebration every February. A kick-off party occurs at the beginning of the month (usually in an area shopping mall), and one fun family event is scheduled each day during the month.

- Organizations in Georgetown, Texas, have learned that there's strength in numbers. Many groups worked together to create a six-week summer enrichment program called "Kid City" for children from kindergarten through 5th grade. The community's parks and recreation department organized and planned activities. The school district donated food. Each week, a different congregation provided volunteers to help with the program. A local volunteer agency coordinated the volunteers, and the community's asset-building initiative managed the funding.

- Town meetings in Mankato, Minnesota, brought residents together to create a list of their shared values, norms, hopes, and dreams for children. To make it easier for all people to attend, the city provided free childcare and bus transportation.

- In Maine, the communities of Kennebunk and Kennebunkport held a parent fair to build children's assets. A local author was invited to speak and raise awareness about the 40 developmental assets.

- Coordinators of the asset-building initiative in Winona, Minnesota, realized that parents—especially working parents and single parents—don't have much extra time or money for parent workshops. So parent educators set up free training sessions during lunch hours at workplaces throughout the city. Coordinators worked closely with company managers to make sure that employees knew about the programs and were encouraged to attend. Educators were pleased by the great number of parents who turned out to improve their parenting skills and learn more about the 40 developmental assets. The community initiative also publishes a "Children's Asset of the Month" flyer, featuring tips on ways adults can build one particular asset in children.

- Organizations interested in children (such as the YMCA, the YWCA, Camp Fire, the Church Council of Greater Seattle, and other groups) joined together to start an asset-building initiative in Seattle, Washington. The initiative was named "It's About Time . . . For Kids" and got many people involved in helping children.

- Asset-builders in Anoka County, Minnesota, worked with a local television station to create an event called "Care About Kids." The all-day event included activities, games, speakers, workshops, ideas for home projects, and a 100-booth resource fair.

- In Dodgeville, Wisconsin, community members come together to let children know they care. "Safe Night in Wisconsin" events throughout the year help build assets and intergenerational relationships. Children and adults meet for activities and discussions on topics like "What it takes to be a friend."

- Asset building is an important part of the community hockey program in Bemidji, Minnesota. "Our programs are purposely noncompetitive," says Carol Anne Johnson, who coordinates the "Healthy Community-Healthy Kids" initiative. "Asset building means providing resources to all kids. If kids know our programs are meant to be fun, they'll come."

- Glenwood Springs, Colorado, has a special focus on younger children through their "Building Assets in Children—Infants, Toddlers, and Preschoolers" program. Parent educators visit the homes of new parents to teach them ways to make asset building a part of their parenting style.

- In Duluth, Minnesota, 11-year-olds can be part of a program called "Incredible Exchange." Participating children are matched with a mentor who's been trained in ways to build assets. Together, the kids and mentors volunteer in nursing homes, hospitals, museums, city parks, or for other organizations. Once participants complete 50 hours of service over several months, they receive coupons for special activities such as karate lessons, ski or golf passes, or music lessons.

BUILDING ASSETS IN OTHER WAYS

Many states have developed special programs to help children grow and thrive. Some of these initiatives use the 40 assets developed by Search Institute, while others don't. But all are doing things that help children succeed:

- Connecticut is working to make asset-building programs a part of childcare centers across the state.

- A program set up by the state legislature in Iowa helps individuals make asset building an important part of their communities.

- The Hawaii "After-School Plus (A+) Program" provides low-cost after-school care to children in every school district in the state. The program, which is available for kids in kindergarten through 6th grade, is offered free to families who otherwise could not afford it. Others pay a flat fee of $25 a month.

- In Minnesota, mayors involved in the League of Minnesota Cities developed concrete ideas on how local city governments can build each of the 40 developmental assets.

- Nationally, the YMCA released the "Nation's Report Card: Assessing Risks to the American Family" in December 1998.

National executive director David R. Mercer called on the nation and its leaders to take seven corrective actions. The first action: "Provide developmental assets children need to thrive."

It isn't necessary to have a fancy organization, a committee, or anyone's permission to start building assets. We can build children's assets in our homes, our neighborhoods, our schools, our childcare centers, and our preschools. We can build assets in our congregations, our businesses, our libraries, our organizations, and our health clinics. We can build assets in our communities, our states, our nation, and our world. We can build assets everywhere.

The important thing is to *begin*. So let's build assets in children. Let's get started right now.

RESOURCES

Understanding how children develop is important in building assets. Here's a list of resources that can teach you the basics. We've also included resources specifically designed to help you understand and build developmental assets. Use these suggestions as a starting point.

RESOURCES FOR UNDERSTANDING YOUNG CHILDREN (BIRTH TO AGE 5)

Caring for Your Baby and Young Child: Birth to Age 5 by the American Academy of Pediatrics (New York: Bantam, 1993). This book gives detailed information, with chapters focusing on specific ages. In addition to heath issues, the authors discuss family issues, childcare, and dealing with children's behavior.

Your Baby and Child: From Birth to Age Five by Penelope Leach (New York: Knopf, 1997). This newly revised edition explores each developmental stage: newborn, settled baby, older baby, toddler, and young child. Includes recent findings from the field and suggestions on how to handle eating, crying, playing, and sleeping.

RESOURCES FOR UNDERSTANDING INFANTS (BIRTH TO 12 MONTHS)

Infants and Mothers: Differences in Development by T. Berry Brazelton, M.D. (New York: Delacorte, 1983). Dr. Brazelton presents his findings from the Child Developmental Unit at the Boston Children's Hospital Medical Center on differences in development among infants and how those differences connect with the personality of the caretaker.

The Psychological Birth of the Human Infant: Symbiosis and Individuation by Margaret S. Mahler, Fred Pine, and Anni Bergman (New York: Basic Books, 1975). This book tells what Mahler and her colleagues learned from observing infants and their mothers during the first two years of life to determine how the very young child develops a capacity for separateness and becomes an individual.

What to Expect the First Year by Arlene Eisenberg, Heidi E. Murkoff, and Sandee E. Hathaway, B.S.N. (New York: Workman Publishing, 1989). A comprehensive month-by-month guide to what parents can expect (and how to respond) as babies develop.

RESOURCES FOR UNDERSTANDING TODDLERS (AGES 13 TO 35 MONTHS)

Baby Steps: The "Whys" of Your Child's Behavior in the First Two Years by Claire B. Kopp, Ph.D., and Donne L. Bean (New York: W.H. Freeman & Company, 1993). This book gives an overview of the first two years of life and how toddlers change emotionally, physically, intellectually, and socially.

The Emotional Life of the Toddler by Alicia F. Lieberman, Ph.D. (New York: Free Press, 1995). This is one of the first books to explore the intense emotional life of toddlers. It gives practical ways to respond to toddlers of different temperaments.

Toddlers and Parents: A Declaration of Independence by T. Berry Brazelton, M.D. (New York: Delta, 1989). Offers concrete ways to survive—and enjoy—the struggles and progress of toddlers.

What to Expect: The Toddler Years by Arlene Eisenberg, Heidi E. Murkoff, and Sandee E. Hathaway, B.S.N. (New York: Workman Publishing, 1994). This guide gives information on what to expect from 13 months to 36 months. It also includes an extensive section on toddler care, health, and safety.

RESOURCES FOR UNDERSTANDING PRESCHOOLERS (AGES 3 TO 5 YEARS)

The Preschool Years: Family Strategies that Work by Ellen Galinsky (New York: Times Books, 1988). From suggesting how to handle routines at home and away from home to developing relationships with preschool-age children, this book looks at key issues that children at this age face.

Raising Preschoolers: Parenting for Today by Sylvia Rimm, Ph.D. (New York: Random House, 1997). This book suggests ways to create an enriching environment for preschoolers while also giving specific ideas on how to handle a wide range of behavior issues.

RESOURCES FOR UNDERSTANDING ELEMENTARY-AGE CHILDREN (AGES 6 TO 11 YEARS)

Caring for Your School-Age Child: Ages 5 to 12 by the American Academy of Pediatrics (New York: Bantam, 1995). This comprehensive book details what's normal and what's not, pointing out the importance of these formative years.

Playground Politics by Stanley I. Greenspan, M.D., and Jacqueline Salmon (Reading, MA: Perseus Books, 1994). In addition to giving the five principles of healthy parenting, the authors show the emotional milestones of grade-school children.

RESOURCES FOR UNDERSTANDING CHILD DEVELOPMENT AND CHILDREN'S ASSETS

All Kids Are Our Kids: What Communities Must Do to Raise Caring and Responsible Children and Adolescents by Peter L. Benson, Ph.D. (San Francisco: Jossey-Bass Publishers, 1997). This book by Search Institute's president outlines the asset vision and how to transform communities for asset building.

The Asset Approach (Minneapolis: Search Institute, 1997). This eight-page brochure presents basic research and other information about assets and asset building. Available in English and Spanish.

Assets: The Magazine of Ideas for Healthy Communities & Healthy Youth (Minneapolis: Search Institute). This quarterly magazine gives real-life stories, concrete ideas, and thought-provoking insights about asset building.

Developmental Assets: A Synthesis of the Scientific Research on Adolescent Development by Peter C. Scales, Ph.D., and Nancy Leffert, Ph.D. (Minneapolis: Search Institute, 1999). This foundational volume examines more than 800 scientific articles and reports on adolescent development that tie to each of the 40 developmental assets.

A Fragile Foundation: The State of Developmental Assets among American Youth by Peter L. Benson, Ph.D., Peter C. Scales, Ph.D., Nancy Leffert, Ph.D., and Eugene C. Roehlkepartain (Minneapolis: Search Institute, 1999). This report looks at 6th to 12th graders today, based on Search Institute's research on almost 100,000 young people in 213 communities.

101 Asset-Building Actions Poster (Minneapolis: Search Institute). A full-color, glossy poster with ideas on how individuals and organizations can build assets. Features key words and phrases in Spanish.

"150 Ways to Show Kids You Care" by Jolene L. Roehlkepartain (Minneapolis: Search Institute, 1996). This unique handout inspires and motivates individuals with practical ideas for showing kids they care. Published in English and in Spanish.

Starting Out Right: Developmental Assets for Children by Nancy Leffert, Ph.D., Peter L. Benson, Ph.D., and Jolene L. Roehlkepartain (Minneapolis: Search Institute, 1997). This in-depth report offers the framework for understanding and building the foundation that children from birth through age 11 need to begin a healthy life. It includes extensive information and research on the impact of each asset on children.

Taking Asset Building Personally: An Action and Reflection Workbook by Jolene L. Roehlkepartain (Minneapolis: Search Institute, 1999). This practical workbook helps people from all walks of life explore their own role in asset building. A companion planning and facilitator's guide gives step-by-step scripts for leading small-group discussions on asset building.

What Kids Need to Succeed by Peter L. Benson, Ph.D., Judy Galbraith, M.A., and Pamela Espeland (Minneapolis: Free Spirit Publishing, 1998). This quick, practical guide gives hundreds of ideas for building assets in 6th to 12th graders at home, in schools, in congregations, and in the community.

What Teens Need to Succeed by Peter L. Benson, Ph.D., Judy Galbraith, M.A., and Pamela Espeland (Minneapolis: Free Spirit

Publishing, 1998). A resource full of ideas, this book inspires and empowers teenagers to build their own developmental assets.

You Can Make a Difference for Kids (Minneapolis: Search Institute, 1999). This eight-page booklet introduces people to the concept of asset building. It gives ideas on how to build assets in children from birth to age 18, and includes tear-out cards that list the 40 developmental assets for each age group.

Resources for Building Assets in Children with Special Needs

The Child with Special Needs: Encouraging Intellectual and Emotional Growth by Stanley I. Greenspan, M.D., Serena Weider, Ph.D., and Robin Simon (New York: Addison Wesley, 1998). This comprehensive guide offers parents specific ways to help their children with special needs reach their full potential.

The Hyperactive Child, Adolescent, and Adult: Attention Deficit Disorder Through the Lifespan by Paul H. Wender, M.D. (New York: Oxford University Press, 1987). This book examines how attention deficit disorder affects a person from childhood through adolescence and adulthood.

Learning Disabilities: A to Z by Corinne Smith, Ph.D., and Lisa Strick (New York: Simon & Schuster, 1997). This book looks at learning disabilities for children ages 3 and older. It offers warning signs, different forms of assessments, and appropriate ways to guide a child with a learning disability through childhood.

The Misunderstood Child: Understanding and Coping with Your Child's Learning Disabilities by Larry B. Silver, M.D. (New York: Times Books, 1998). This third edition gives parents of children with learning disabilities a full understanding of positive, effective treatment strategies to use at home and at school.

Parents' Complete Special Education Guide by Roger Pierangelo and Robert Jacoby (New York: Prentice Hall, 1995). This book offers tips, techniques, and pertinent information on how to help a child with special needs get the best and most appropriate education.

Putting on the Brakes: Young People's Guide to Understanding Attention Deficit Hyperactivity Disorder by Patricia O. Quinn and Judith M. Stern (Washington, DC: Magination Press, 1991). A book that explores attention deficit hyperactivity disorder (ADHD) in detail and suggests ways to deal with it.

The School Survival Guide for Kids with LD and *The Survival Guide for Kids with LD* by Gary Fisher, Ph.D., and Rhoda Cummings, Ed.D. (Minneapolis: Free Spirit Publishing, 1991, 1990). These two books provide tips and strategies to make learning easier and more fun for children with learning differences.

Teaching Kids with Learning Difficulties in the Regular Classroom by Susan Winebrenner (Minneapolis: Free Spirit Publishing, 1996). Gives practical ways to help students labeled "special," "slow," or "LD."

Resources for Building Assets in Gifted Children

Bringing Out the Best: A Resource Guide for Parents of Young Gifted Children by Jacqulyn Saunders with Pamela Espeland (Minneapolis: Free Spirit Publishing, 1991). Geared for parents of children ages 2–7, this comprehensive guide focuses on the special needs of gifted children.

The Gifted Kids' Survival Guide: A Teen Handbook by Judy Galbraith, M.A., and Jim Delisle, Ph.D. (Minneapolis: Free Spirit Publishing, 1996). This revised edition is the ultimate guide for helping gifted young people survive and thrive in a world that doesn't always value, support, or understand high ability.

Growing Up Gifted: Developing the Potential of Children at Home and at School by Barbara Clark (New York: Merrill, 1997). This fifth edition is one of the most thorough in regards to gifted children. It is used in many college classes.

How to Develop Your Child's Gifts and Talents During the Elementary Years by RaeLynne P. Rein, Ph.D., and Rachel Rein (Los Angeles: Lowell House, 1994). Helps parents identify and nurture gifts of leadership, creativity, humor, and social consciousness.

Managing the Social and Emotional Needs of the Gifted by Connie C. Schmitz, Ph.D., and Judy Galbraith, M.A. (Free Spirit Publishing, 1985). Over 30 concrete, easy-to-use strategies help gifted students develop socially and emotionally as well as intellectually.

Parents' Guide to Raising a Gifted Child: Recognizing and Developing Your Child's Potential from Preschool to Adolescence by James Alvino, Ph.D., and the editors of *Gifted Children Monthly* (New York: Little, Brown and Co., 1985). This comprehensive parenting book examines all developmental areas of gifted children. The authors also wrote *Parents' Guide to Raising a Gifted Toddler: Recognizing and Developing the Potential of Your Child from Birth to Five Years* (New York: Little, Brown and Co., 1989).

OTHER RESOURCES FOR BUILDING ASSETS

Beyond Leaf Raking by Eugene C. Roehlkepartain (Nashville: Abingdon Press, 1993). Based on research on service learning, this book challenges congregations to involve young people in educationally challenging community service.

Building Assets in Congregations by Eugene C. Roehlkepartain (Minneapolis: Search Institute, 1998). This in-depth book offers everything on how to create an asset-building congregation. Includes worksheets, tips, and 10 reproducible bulletin inserts.

Building Assets Together by Jolene L. Roehlkepartain (Minneapolis: Search Institute, 1997). Gives creative, easy-to-use activities to introduce developmental assets. Includes 94 interactive group activities for 6th- to 12th-grade students and 41 reproducible worksheets.

Creating Intergenerational Community by Jolene L. Roehlkepartain (Minneapolis: Search Institute, 1996). A booklet with 75 easy ideas for building relationships between children and adults.

The Healthy Communities • Healthy Youth Booklet (Minneapolis: Search Institute, 1998). This 20-page informational booklet paints a comprehensive yet easy-to-understand picture of the asset-building framework and its implications for communities.

The Healthy Communities • Healthy Youth Tool Kit (Minneapolis: Search Institute, 1998). This guide includes more than 300 examples of how communities are building assets in young people. It also includes guidelines and practical tips on how to launch and sustain a community-wide asset-building effort.

Ideas for Parents: Newsletter Master Set by Jolene L. Roehlkepartain (Minneapolis: Search Institute, 1997). This set of 50 newsletter masters lets concerned adults provide parents with practical tips on how they can help their children grow into responsible, successful adults.

Learning and Living: How Asset Building for Youth Can Unify a School's Mission by Donald Draayer and Eugene C. Roehlkepartain (Minneapolis: Search Institute, 1998). This short booklet shows how superintendents, principals, teachers, counselors, and other school staff can understand their role as asset builders from a perspective of total student development.

Parenting with a Purpose: A Positive Approach for Raising Confident, Caring Youth by Dean Feldmeyer and Eugene C. Roehlkepartain (Minneapolis: Search Institute, 1998). Introduces adults to asset-based parenting and gives practical ideas on getting started.

Pass It On: Ready-to-Use Handouts for Asset Builders (Minneapolis: Search Institute, 1999). This set includes 91 asset-building handout masters for many audiences.

Sharing the Asset Message Speaker's Kit (Minneapolis: Search Institute, 1997). Includes a detailed script, colorful overheads, and ready-to-copy handouts for presentations about asset building.

Tapping the Potential: Discovering Congregations' Role in Building Assets by Glenn A. Seefeldt and Eugene C. Roehlkepartain (Minneapolis: Search Institute, 1997). This short booklet presents key ideas about asset building in congregations.

PUBLISHERS OF ASSET-BUILDING MATERIALS

Search Institute has developed the framework of the 40 developmental assets and has a number of asset-building publications, videos, and reproducible handouts. Search Institute's Web site has a wide array of information on assets and asset building, including examples of how parents, educators, congregations, and communities are building assets in children and youth. To request a catalog, contact Search at:

Search Institute
700 South Third Street, Suite 210
Minneapolis, MN 55415-1138
Toll-free phone: 1-800-888-7828
In Minneapolis and St. Paul: (612) 376-8955
Email: si@search-institute.org
Web site: *www.search-institute.org/*

Free Spirit Publishing, founded in 1983, specializes in books and learning materials for kids, parents, and teachers. Many of Free Spirit's books address practical ways to build developmental assets. To request a catalog, contact Free Spirit at:

Free Spirit Publishing Inc.
400 First Avenue North, Suite 616
Minneapolis, MN 55401-1724
Toll-free phone: 1-800-735-7323
In Minneapolis and St. Paul: (612) 338-2068
Email: help4kids@freespirit.com
Web site: *www.freespirit.com*

INDEX

ABOUT THE AUTHORS

Jolene L. Roehlkepartain is a parent educator, author, and speaker on family and children's issues. She is the founder of Ideas Ink, a communications consulting company that focuses on parenting, children's issues, youth development, and education. She is a former magazine editor who launched two national magazines, *Adoptive Families* and *Children's Ministry*, and has worked with children through recreation and congregational programs. Ms. Roehlkepartain is the author of 12 books, including *Fidget Busters, Taking Asset Building Personally, An Asset Builder's Guide to Youth and Money, Teaching Kids to Care and Share*, and *Building Assets Together*. She speaks on children's assets and is the coauthor of *Starting Out Right: Developmental Assets for Children*. She lives in Minneapolis, Minnesota, with her husband and two children, ages 3 and 9.

Nancy Leffert, Ph.D., is a researcher, author, and speaker with expertise in child and adolescent development. She is Associate Dean at The Fielding Institute in Santa Barbara, California, and Adjunct Senior Fellow at Search Institute in Minneapolis, Minnesota. She earned her doctorate in child psychology from the Institute of Child Development at the University of Minnesota and a master's degree in social work from San Diego State University. She is interested in the effects of community contexts on child and adolescent development and factors that contribute to healthy development, particularly as they pertain to special populations, such as young people with attention deficit disorders, learning disabilities, and affective disorders. Dr. Leffert is a licensed independent clinical social worker and the former director of a child and youth learning problems clinic. She is the author of many articles and book chapters on development and the coauthor of several Search Institute books including *Starting Out Right: Developmental Assets for Children, Developmental Assets: A Synthesis of the Scientific Research on Adolescent Development, A Fragile Foundation: The State of Developmental Assets among American Youth*, and *Making the Case: Measuring the Impact of Youth Development Programs*. She is married and has two children, ages 18 and 21. She lives in Santa Barbara, California.

OTHER GREAT BOOKS FROM FREE SPIRIT

A Leader's Guide to What Young Children Need to Succeed
Working Together to Build Assets from Birth to Age 11
by Jolene L. Roehlkepartain and Nancy Leffert, Ph.D.
Ready-to-use workshops for parents, educators, and other adults who work with children from birth through grade 6.
$14.95; 96 pp.; softcover; 8½" x 11"

What Kids Need to Succeed
Proven, Practical Ways to Raise Good Kids
Revised, Expanded, and Updated Edition
by Peter L. Benson, Ph.D., Judy Galbraith, M.A., and Pamela Espeland
Our new edition of a proven best-seller identifies 40 developmental "assets" kids need to lead healthy, productive, positive lives, then gives them more than 900 suggestions for building their own assets wherever they are. *Parents' Choice* approved. For parents, teachers, community and youth leaders, and teens.
$5.99; 256 pp.; softcover; 4⅛" x 6⅞"

What Teens Need to Succeed
Proven, Practical Ways to Shape Your Own Future
by Peter L. Benson, Ph.D., Judy Galbraith, M.A., and Pamela Espeland
Based on a national survey, this book describes 40 developmental "assets" all teens need to succeed in life, then gives hundreds of suggestions teens can use to build assets wherever they are. For ages 11 & up.
$14.95; 368 pp.; softcover; illus.; 7¼" x 9¼"

To place an order or to request a free catalog of SELF–HELP FOR KIDS® and SELF–HELP FOR TEENS® materials, please write, call, email, or visit our Web site:

Free Spirit Publishing Inc.
400 First Avenue North • Suite 616 • Minneapolis, MN 55401-1724
toll-free 800.735.7323 • local 612.338.2068 • fax 612.337.5050
help4kids@freespirit.com • www.freespirit.com